PICKLE, PEPPER, AND TIP-IN, TOO

KEVIN NELSON

55,245

A FIRESIDE BOOK
PUBLISHED BY
SIMON & SCHUSTER

NEW YORK   LONDON
TORONTO   SYDNEY   TOKYO
SINGAPORE

FIRESIDE
Rockefeller Center
1230 Avenue of the Americas
New York, New York 10020

Copyright © 1994 by Kevin Nelson

FIRESIDE and colophon are registered trademarks of
Simon & Schuster Inc.

DESIGNED BY BARBARA M. MARKS
Manufactured in the United States of America

10   9   8   7   6   5   4   3   2   1

Library of Congress Cataloging-in-Publication Data
Nelson, Kevin, date.
    Pickle, pepper, and tip-in, too / Kevin Nelson.
        p.   cm.
    "A Fireside book."
    1. Ball games—Rules—Juvenile literature.   2. Sports—Rules—
Juvenile literature.   [1. Ball games—Rules.   2. Sports—Rules.]
I. Title.
GV861.N45   1994
796.3—dc20   94-6407
                                                              CIP
                                                              AC

ISBN: 0-671-87956-1

"Ludileges variari volant."*

—Francisco Cervantes de Salazar

* Vary the rules according to the desires of the players.

To Dave,
who always brought me along,
and to Mark C.,
for all the games we played together.

CONTENTS

PREFACE

Before I started work on this book my editor gave me one instruction: Make it fun. What good is a book about games, she reasoned, if it isn't fun?

Indeed. This book is a lot about games, and a little bit about growing up. Many adults will recognize a piece of their childhood in some of the games that are described in this book.

This is intentional. Another goal of this book—besides being fun—was to record some of the games played by previous generations of children, as a means of keeping those games alive. Some games like Work-ups and One Old Cat appear to have lost their appeal with today's young people, and yet they deserve to be remembered.

One way to remember a game is to put it in a book, and that's what I've done here. There are more than 250 games in this book, not including variations and the variations on the variations. This is a lot of games, although I will be the first to admit that one volume alone hardly exhausts the subject. Not even ten volumes of this size would exhaust the subject. Games are like children. As long as we keep making the latter, we are going to continue to have fresh examples of the former.

The major goal of this book is to help children learn the skills of sports—baseball, soccer, tennis, hockey, etc.—by playing games derived from them. I wanted to include as many of the games being played today, by the current generation of young people, as I could find. Their parents may never have played Kickback, Knockout, or Wall Ball, but their children certainly play them, and these games are in here too.

Ideally this book will be a source of new games and new inspirations for parents, teachers, camp counselors, and coaches. Adults who work with young people are always looking for new ways of doing things, new ways to engage the attention of people whose attentions are constantly shifting, and it is my ardent hope that this book will be useful to them.

The importance of games in a child's physical and social development cannot be overstated. If this book can somehow contribute to this process, if it helps a parent think of a game to play with his or her child or a coach to find fun ways to teach basic skills or to liven up a practice, then I will have achieved much of what I set out to do.

This is a book of sports-derived games: games that children can play when they're not playing the sport itself. It is intended for children between the ages of six and thirteen, beginning at the age when boys and girls leave behind the games of infancy and turn their attention to team sports and group activities. I have tried to include as many different sports and games as I could, appealing to all kinds of children, playing in a variety of environments. No one should feel left out.

Bowing to the realities of contemporary life, it is assumed that most of these games will be supervised. For many of the games, it is assumed that an adult will be present. If there is one major difference between today's games-players and those of past generations, it is this: Children don't tend to play on their own as much. Everything is supervised. The reasons for this are many and complex, and beyond the scope of this book. But it is truly a sad commentary when our children, for whatever reason, can't simply go out and play. As a hockey instructor told me, "Kids can't be kids anymore."

Assuming that adults will supervise these games, the write-ups are largely directed to them. A certain level of sports knowledge is nice, but not mandatory. Anyone with enthusiasm and a love of playing can use these games to help their children get started in sports. But I am certainly not trying to talk over anyone's head. As an author I would feel greatly encouraged, even thrilled, if young people decided to crack open the covers of this book to see if they could find something good in it.

If they do, they will find a great many games that they can play without any old folks around. This was also one of my aims: to include a batch of games that young people can play on their own, free of parental supervision, with little or no equipment. Every young person who loves sports and loves to play games should draw inspiration from the story of John Daly, the professional golfer and PGA champion. When he was young, Daly collected balls from golf course water hazards. Then he took the balls over to a local baseball diamond and hit them over the backstop. In this manner, Daly learned to hit a golf ball longer and straighter than any person alive.

Though his driving range may have been a bit offbeat, there's nothing unusual about what Daly did. Circumstances force children to play a game in a way that varies from the established rules, so they make up a variation, or an entirely new game, that suits them better. It is not just famous athletes who do this, every child does. So, for that matter, do parents, teachers, coaches, youth counselors, and anybody else who works with children. Games are as organic as moist clay. As long as people are having fun and receiving joy from the process, they should feel free to push and pound and squeeze their games into any shape they want.

THE ART OF GAMES,
OR HOW TO USE, ENJOY, AND
BENEFIT FROM THIS BOOK

This book contains more than 250 sports-oriented games for active children between the ages of six and thirteen. In order for them to get the most benefit from this book, their parents, coaches, supervisors, teachers, grandparents, guardians, and camp counselors may care to observe the following guidelines:

Do not get hung up over rules.

This book is like a cookbook, a cookbook for games. People may follow these recipes to the letter, or they may not. In general, they should feel free to change the rules of the game to fit the situation. An overzealous attachment to the rules will stifle a child's natural creativity and joy.

If a game works, use it. If it doesn't, don't.

Games are like jazz, to use another metaphor—full of improvisation and spur-of-the-moment creativity. Improvise with these games. If one game isn't working, go to another. Just blow, cat, blow.

A person does not need lots of money or fancy equipment to play games.

The best games are the simplest. The best games require only an active imagination and the willingness to try. The geography of games is virtually limitless. The street and public park are as good as the country club. This book has made a special effort to include all sorts of games for children between the ages of six and thirteen, for all ability levels, playing in a variety of environments.

Time is relative when playing games.

Some games last a half hour, some a half minute. The time it takes to play a game depends on any number of variables: how many players there are, their ages and abilities, the difficulty of the game, the objectives of the coaches and players, even the time of day. The benefit of a game isn't measured by the amount of time it takes. Even a game of only five minutes can make the difference between a dull practice and an exciting one.

Don't go too fast. Don't go too slow.

An adult playing these games with young children might be wise to start with low expectations. Setting your sights too high may put too much pressure on the players and set the stage for disappointment—yours and theirs. That said, it is never a good idea to underestimate the capabilities of young people. Give a young person a challenge and he or she will almost always respond to it. The best rule is: *Be flexible.*

Follow a building-block approach to teaching games.

Every sport teaches its younger players in essentially the same way, gradually building or layering on skills. One skill is combined with another skill and in this way the player learns and progresses. This book works on the same principle. Each chapter begins with the easiest of games, ideal for younger players. The games grow progressively harder and more complicated, requiring combinations of skills and working together as a team.

Use the difficulty ratings only as a guidepost.

Each game in the book has been assigned a level of difficulty. These ratings are meant only as a rough guideline. Some children may find the advanced games a snap while stumbling on the less difficult ones. The "easy" rating denotes a good game for beginners that just one or two people can play. Advanced games frequently have more complicated rules and require more players and equipment.

Don't disregard an easier game.

Coaches and parents should not scorn the easier games. They can be a pleasant change of pace for older children. Playing an easier game may also be an effective way to commingle age groups.

If possible, let the older children teach the younger ones.

Childhood development studies have shown that children derive great benefits from cooperative learning. The more advanced child learns while teaching the less advanced one. Children all have different skills, and mixing abilities and ages can bring these qualities into the open. Children also enjoy learning from other children. A child may have a way of phrasing a piece of advice that an adult wouldn't think of, and this might enhance the learning process.

Be willing to experiment with the ball.

It only makes sense that the balls used by adults or fully developed teen-agers may not be right for younger people. Is the ball too big? Try a smaller one. Too heavy? Try a lighter one. Or perhaps the ball is too small. Try a bigger, lighter one. In volleyball, for instance, many coaches begin with balloons and beach balls before moving up to softer volley-balls. Young baseball players now use balls made entirely of cloth. The trend in recent years toward "age-appropriate" balls and equipment is truly a wonderful thing.

Do not stick exclusively to the games in one sport.

Every youngster can enjoy and benefit from the games of other sports, not just the ones from his or her favorite sport. Truly every child, at heart, is a Bo Jackson—a person capable of playing, or at least enjoying, more than one sport. Forcing a youngster to choose a single sport will produce a burned-out, unhappy child.

A game by any other name is still a game.

Different parts of the country, like different generations, have different names for the same game. It is very possible that people will recognize some of the games in this book, but have grown up calling them some-thing else. This is entirely in keeping with the nature of games. Like folk tales, they are continually changing and adapting to fit the wants and needs of the people who are playing them.

Be safe.

Games aren't fun if someone gets hurt. Use the proper equipment, and make sure the field of play is a safe one. It is impossible, in a book of this kind, to specify what is safe and what is not in all cases. Even when children are wearing all the latest equipment, they can do unsafe things. The best piece of safety equipment, for children and adults alike, is common sense. Always err on the side of safety.

Be positive.

Sports is a tremendously positive environment for young people, especially considering all the other challenges they face in life these days. Don't poison this atmosphere with negativity. Encourage; don't criticize.

Winning at all costs isn't very much fun.

The games in this book seek to foster the healthiest attitudes of team sports—cooperation, good-natured competition, selflessness, shared sacrifice—while building practical skills in a fun way. Fun, not winning and losing, should be the fundamental principle behind teaching young people how to play sports. If young people are not enjoying themselves, they are going to get bored or disillusioned and quit. Then, everyone loses.

Competition doesn't necessarily mean keeping score.

Being able to compete against other people in a game of one's choosing is one of the great joys of sports. Competition helps people learn and grow. Almost every drill can be enhanced by introducing incentives, or the element of competition. But when playing a game, it is not always necessary to keep score in order for children to receive the benefits of good-natured competition.

Everybody plays.

Every child, even the less gifted ones, should be allowed to participate fully in the games. An important related rule: Adults should pick the teams, rather than the children, to ensure that the different levels of players are divided equally and fairly.

Don't overcoach and overparent.

Nothing can spoil a child's enjoyment quicker than an overbearing coach or parent. Parents must be willing to let a coach do things his or her way. Coaches must be willing to listen to helpful suggestions from parents genuinely concerned about the welfare of their children. In other words, be sensitive to what's best for the children. If parents, coaches, spectators, and other adults involved in youth athletics would truly understand, and accept, this simple rule, so many of the problems associated with youth sports would disappear in a wink.

See this book as a collection of ideas.

This is not just a book of games, it is a book of ideas. There are over 250 ideas for having fun in this book. Each game represents an idea. Each idea is nothing more than a starting point for an imaginative mind, or two or three imaginative minds, or dozens of imaginative minds, acting together in pursuit of fun. So much has changed for young people today, but they share one common trait with all the kids who have ever lived in the whole history of the world: They love to have fun.

PICKLE, PEPPER, AND TIP-IN, TOO

ONE

BADMINTON

ost Americans regard badminton as something to do while the steaks are sizzling on the barbecue. They set the nets up very high, and bat the little shuttlecock back and forth between sips of iced tea and snippets of idle conversation.

The sport of badminton is something else entirely. It is a rapid-fire, quick-reaction game that provides an athletic alternative to children who may be crowded out of the more traditional (and rougher) after-school sports. Badminton appeals to a different sort of athlete, and engenders a different sort of approach. Trying to "kill" the shuttlecock—a tactic often endorsed by large-limbed males—will produce few dividends when the opponent is a skilled player. Power is not paramount in badminton; quickness is. And every child can receive some benefit from this hugely entertaining activity.

The most critical element in any badminton match is the net. It makes the difference between sport and idle amusement. The net should not be set high, like a volleyball net. High nets are the bane of the game. They have helped give badminton its unfair "sissy" image, because they allow players to hit high, looping shots that carve gentle parabolas in the sky and require little effort to return. Set the net at about five feet, from the ground to the top, and play the game for keeps. Boom! Smash! Pow! Wham! Slam!

BALLOONMINTON

Players: 2 or 4
Area: Playground, gym, yard
Equipment: Badminton rackets, balloons, net and poles
Level of Difficulty: Easy

Badminton does not use a ball; instead, players bat little plastic shuttlecocks over the net. These things can really fly. They dip and dart and dance as the players scurry about hitting backhands, overhead smashes, lunging saves, and lightly touched drops. A simple flick of the wrist in badminton can produce astonishing results.

Nevertheless, the speed and shiftiness with which a shuttlecock moves can take some getting used to, especially for the very young. A gentle way to ease younger children into the game is by playing with a balloon—perhaps with a little water in it to add some weight. They can play ordinary badminton rules, either singles or doubles. Only the serving side can score. Games go up to 15, and must be won by 2 points.

NO NET

Players: 6–12
Area: Yard, playground, gym, beach, park
Equipment: Badminton rackets, shuttlecock
Level of Difficulty: Easy–moderate

No Net is an unusual badminton game because, as the name implies, it does not require a net. As a result, No Net can be played almost anywhere, from the backyard to the beach.

The game does, however, require boundaries of some sort. A line should divide the two teams, and the shuttlecock must go beyond the line to be considered a fair hit. Slams are not allowed. The shuttlecock must always head upward after leaving a player's racket, never down.

To ensure that everyone participates, divide the group into two teams—the even numbers and the odd numbers. Each player is assigned a number and takes his or her turn accordingly. No. 1 hits across to No. 2, who hits back to No. 3, who returns to No. 4, and so forth. If a player misses or hits out, he or she leaves the game and everyone's numbers change correspondingly. The last person remaining wins the game.

SOLO BADMINTON

Players: 1
Area: Yard, playground, gym
Equipment: Badminton racket, shuttlecock, net and poles
Level of Difficulty: Easy–moderate

What does a young badminton enthusiast do if there's no one around to play with? How about Solo Badminton? The player starts on one side of the net and hits it over, then runs under the net and hits it back. Then he runs under the net, hits it back again, runs, hits, runs, hits, runs, and—if he is up to it—hits once more. To an adult, all this running and hitting may seem an impossible task, but the enterprising child who avoids the deep hit and keeps the shuttlecock high can stage an excellent competition against himself.

SHUTTLE

Players: 5 or more
Area: Yard, playground, gym
Equipment: Badminton rackets, shuttlecock, net and poles
Level of Difficulty: Easy–moderate

Shuttle is the badminton version of the famous tennis game Around the World. Players divide into two groups. Each group lines up at the back of the court single-file on each side of the net.

Shuttle combines running with quick reactions. The first person in line hits, then runs to his or her right around the net to the end of the line on the opposite side. The opposite line returns. Each person in line does this (or tries to): hits, then shuttles around to the line on the opposite side.

Other ways to play: A simpler version of Shuttle for younger players is to have each player run to the back of the same line, rather than to the opposite side of the net. A more competitive version eliminates players who make a bad shot or miss. Players are gradually eliminated until two finalists remain, and they play a 1-point match to determine the winner.

RELAY BADMINTON

Players: 4
Area: Yard, playground, gym
Equipment: Badminton rackets, shuttlecock, net and poles
Level of Difficulty: Moderate–advanced

For those looking for a brisk workout, this is an excellent game. It is a doubles game, but instead of protecting a certain area of the court as they do in ordinary doubles, players take turns hitting the shuttlecock. A person cannot hit twice in a row; teammates must alternate. First one hits, then the other, and they scramble around the court working up quite a sweat.

A really fun—and challenging—variation is to require the players on each team to switch rackets after one of them hits. This can be done with two rackets or one.

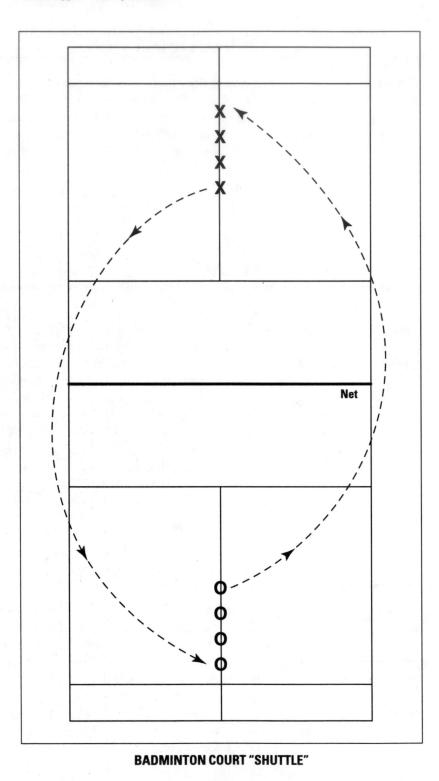

BADMINTON COURT "SHUTTLE"

PICKLE BALL

Players: 2 or 4
Area: Gym
Equipment: Pickle ball rackets, net and poles, Wiffle Ball
Level of Difficulty: Easy

S uch a name! How can anyone not have fun playing a game called Pickle Ball?

One observer described Pickle Ball as "a slowed-down version of tennis." It has many similarities to badminton or paddle tennis as well. It is an indoor game, excellent for small spaces. Like badminton, it is easy to learn and provides a vigorous workout for children who may be turned off by the more traditional sports or even other racket games.

The pickle ball paddle looks like an oversized table tennis paddle. The ball is a Wiffle Ball. A pickle ball court is the size of a doubles badminton court, with a three-foot-high net. The game is usually singles or doubles, although three or four players on a side in informal games is common.

Official Pickle Ball rules stipulate one hit per side, but again, the rules may be stretched to fit the situation. Some P.E. teachers allow three hits per side to give beginning players a feel for the game. Pickle Ball, like badminton, produces fast-paced rallies—Zing! Pop! Pow!—that make the players react and move.

What distinguishes Pickle Ball from other racket games is the seven-foot "non-volley zone" extending across the court on both sides of the net. This innovation prevents players from hovering Gulliver-like around the Lilliputian net and smashing the smithereens out of the ball. Pickle Ball prizes clever shot-making over displays of raw power, although overhead slams are as much a part of the game as passing shots down the line.

Players cannot volley the serve; the Wiffle Ball must bounce. Nor can the server follow up his or her serve with a volley. The server must let his opponents' return bounce once on his side after a serve. Both these rules tend to encourage rallies whenever possible, a primary aim of this pleasant game.

BASEBALL/
SOFTBALL/
TEE BALL

To be successful, young baseball, softball, and tee ball players must learn the basic skills of catching, throwing, and hitting, and the games in this chapter will help them do that.

One of the most positive developments in youth sports in recent years has been the willingness to experiment with different kinds of balls. Many young people are intimidated by the size and hardness of the ball they are being asked to play with. This is true in baseball, soccer, football, volleyball, and basketball. In baseball, as in these other sports, coaches and parents should be encouraged to play with softer and/or larger balls. These "safety baseballs"—balls made of cloth—and other softer balls will allow a young person to stop worrying about the ball itself and enjoy the game.

CATCH

Players: 2
Area: Yard, baseball field, street
Equipment: Softball or baseball, 1 baseball glove for each participant
Level of Difficulty: Easy

Throwing and catching are the primary skills of baseball. In the game of Catch, a player tosses the ball back and forth with another player, who is standing a comfortable distance away. It is a good way to get to know someone or catch up on the news of the day with a friend. It is communication of the most pleasant kind. As the two players toss the ball back and forth, they talk.

For such a simple-seeming game, Catch is endlessly varied. If the field of play allows it and their arms are warm, the pair can gradually extend the distance between them. They will naturally make a game of it, mixing up their throws—now a hard grounder, now a backpedaling fly ball—to give each other harder balls to catch. As several of these baseball skill games show, all a person needs to bring to a game of catch besides a mitt and ball is a little imagination.

21

Players: 2
Area: Yard, baseball field, street
Equipment: Softball or baseball, baseball gloves
Level of Difficulty: Easy

21 is a catch game with points. It is a simple game, best for younger players. It teaches them accuracy and supplies focus to an ordinary game of catch.

The players stand ten to fifteen feet apart, whatever is comfortable for them. They throw the ball back and forth trying to be as accurate as they can. A throw to the chest area—where they should be putting the ball—counts for 2 points. A throw that forces the other person to bend or move his feet, counts for 1 point. A ball that is way off line and cannot be caught at all is minus 2. A person might also be penalized a point for that bad habit of major league outfielders, the nonchalant one-handed catch. As the players grow more skilled they can throw the ball faster. The first player—or team—to make it to 21, wins.

TIRE TOSS

Players: Unlimited
Area: Yard, open area, baseball field
Equipment: Car tire, softball or baseball
Level of Difficulty: Easy

Tire Toss is a spinoff of the old football drill, where a quarterback tests his arm by throwing through the center of a car tire. Instead of a football, the player tosses a baseball through the tire at twenty paces away (or whatever seems appropriate for the size and skill level of the players).

Set the tire on a bucket, to give the thrower a better target, with a fence behind the tire to stop the balls. Points are awarded on a sliding scale. A clean strike through the center of the doughnut earns 10 points; a ball that hits the tire but still goes through, 5 points; simply hitting the tire earns 2. Missing the whole thing, of course, counts for nothing. Each player gets two throws per turn. Players can compete against one another or, what is preferable, put the players all on the same team and let them root for one another to succeed.

LEMONBALL

Players: 5–10
Area: Baseball field, yard, street
Equipment: Wiffle Bat, plastic lemon juice container
Level of Difficulty: Easy

Everybody knows how to play Wiffle Ball. Lemonball is its country cousin. Lemonball players use a Wiffle Bat but play with a different ball. Buy a plastic lemon-shaped lemon juice container. Pour out the contents and replace the cap. *That* is the ball. It acts even loopier than a Wiffle Ball, dipping, dropping, diving, spinning, and seeming to obey not the Laws of Nature but its own quirky gyroscopic rhythms.

FOLLOW THE BOUNCING BALL

Players: 1–2
Area: Yard or along the sidelines of a baseball field
Equipment: Softball or baseball, bat
Level of Difficulty: Easy

Follow the Bouncing Ball lets one person practice hitting skills by himself. He doesn't need anybody else—just those two most splendid companions, a ball and bat.

This is a balancing and reaction game that lets youngsters work on the hand-to-eye coordination so essential to hitting and, indeed, to all sports. Take a bat in one hand, a ball in the other. Balance the ball on the meat end of the bat and start batting the ball in the air, trying to keep it alive. The object is to keep the ball bouncing; every bounce counts 1 point. Someone who scores 50 points—fifty consecutive bounces—is definitely not a person to be trifled with. If there are two players, see which one can do it the most times.

To do this well a player must keep his legs moving and stay alert. In the beginning, he can hold his hands in the middle of the bat next to the trademark. As he gets more proficient, he should move his grip down the handle of the bat. The closer he gets to the end of the bat, the harder it will be to keep the ball alive.

CATCH OVER A HOUSE

CATCH OVER A HOUSE

Players: 2–3
Area: Yard
Equipment: Rubber ball, tennis ball, or softball or baseball; baseball glove (optional)
Level of Difficulty: Easy

Catch Over a House is a game of catch with a house, or other large obstruction such as a car or truck, hedge, or wall, in between. The ball can be a plain rubber ball, a tennis ball, a high-bouncing Super Ball, or a softball or baseball (use gloves). One might also try throwing a football if so inclined.

Catch Over a House situates one player in front of the obstruction, and one player in back. Watch out for windows if you play over a house. Ideally, neither person can see the other, so when the ball appears it comes as a surprise. The players must react instantly and catch it before it hits the ground. They can take nothing for granted, for the ball can come at any time, and their eyes patrol the sky as if they were searching the night for shooting stars.

PICKLE

Players: 3
Area: Yard or grassy
    area
Equipment: Softball or
    baseball, 2 baseball
    gloves, 2 bases
Level of Difficulty: Easy

Pickle hones the skills of throwing and catching while adding a third element: running the bases. The art of stealing bases relies on judgment as much as speed, and Pickle utilizes them both.

There are two fielders and one runner. The runner runs until he is thrown out, at which time he becomes a fielder and the person who tags him becomes the runner.

Set up two bases fifteen to twenty feet apart. The bases cannot be too far apart because the runner must have a sporting chance to make it safely. The bases can be made of anything—an old pillow, a cap, a spare glove, whatever is handy.

The runner tries to get from one base to the other without being thrown out by the two playing catch. Doing this successfully requires equal amounts of pluck and luck. Sooner or later the runner must make a break for it—and when he does, the pickle commences. One fielder chases him backward toward the base where he started, then tosses to the other fielder who chases him toward the base where he dearly wants to go. The runner desperately tries to elude each of the fielders, scampering back and forth, back and forth, until he is tagged, or better yet, slides into the base with a flourish. Safe!

Pickle is the bane of suburban lawns everywhere, as the ceaseless running that the game requires inevitably wears dirt patches and brown spots in grass. Sighing over the effect that Pickle had had on their lawn one summer, a mother of two boys complained to her husband about it. "Sweetheart," he said, "we're not raising grass. We're raising children."

RUN DOWN

Players: 4
Area: Outfield grass of
    baseball field
Equipment: Baseball
    gloves, baseball, 2
    bases
Level of Difficulty:
    Easy–moderate

Run Down is Pickle with focus. Pickle is traditionally a relaxed game that features lots of throws. In Run Down the players more closely simulate an actual pick-off play at first, and try to get the runner out with one throw or none.

There are four players: pitcher, first baseman, second baseman, and runner. The casual back-and-forth throws that characterize most Pickle games should not occur here. With the runner leading off first base, the pitcher throws over and catches him off the bag. (The runner deliberately gets caught off base.) The first baseman then sets off in chase.

In a game situation of this kind, the fewer throws the better. The more throws there are, the more chances there will be for overthrows or something else going wrong. In Run Down, the first baseman must run the runner down and tag him without throwing at all, or make only one toss to the second baseman so that he can tag him. The runner tries to elude the tag, of course, and force lots of throws. The runner has done his job if he can make the first and second basemen toss the ball back and forth between them.

Run Down moves very quickly, since just one throw to first base forces the runner to take off. Everybody rotates positions after one or two outs.

FLIP GAME

Players: Unlimited
Area: Baseball field or open area
Equipment: Baseball gloves for all players, 1 baseball per team
Level of Difficulty: Easy–moderate

The Flip Game gets young players accustomed to catching and quickly flipping a baseball, something that infielders in particular should know how to do. Arrange everybody in a circle, with each individual about ten feet from the next person in the circle. With lots of kids, divide the players into equal groups and form several circles. The object of the game is for the players to flip the ball around the circle as quickly as they can.

The players toss the ball underhanded, pulling it out of their mitts and tossing it to the person next to them in the circle. On the first rotation, go clockwise. When the ball returns to the kid who started, he should start it back around again counterclockwise.

With two (or more) competing groups, see which team can get the ball around the circuit faster. Or make it a counting game. Each time a person touches the ball he sings out a number. The team that has counted the highest at the end of three minutes is the winner.

PEPPER

Players: 3–5
Area: Baseball field
Equipment: Baseball gloves, baseball, bat
Level of Difficulty: Easy–moderate

Pepper is a baseball classic. It's both functional and fun. It's a game that adults can easily step into and not feel out of place, although youngsters can of course play it very well on their own. There is a timeless quality to Pepper. Babe Ruth played it, Kirby Puckett plays it, and the Babe Ruths and Kirby Pucketts of the twenty-first and twenty-second centuries will undoubtedly play it as well.

One person is the batter; the other three or four players are fielders. A Pepper game should never have more than four or five players; too many players ruins its intimacy. The fielders stand a short distance away from the batter and lob soft, easily manageable throws at him. The batter chokes up on the bat and raps the ball back to the fielders—now a grounder, now an easy pop-up. Everything about Pepper is easy. It's a rhythm game. No hard throws, no unnecessary movements. A person throws, the ball pops off the bat, the fielder reacts. Major leaguers often toss the ball using their gloves, not their throwing hands. Pepper is a perfect game before a game because it limbers up the arm and body, and helps people think in terms of playing ball.

It is easy to add a competitive element to Pepper if one desires. Give each hitter twelve swings. At the end of his twelve swings, the first fielder in line takes a turn with the bat. But the fielders must earn this honor. If someone makes an error with the glove or tosses a ball askew to the batter, he goes to the end of the line and has to work his way back up to bat.

BATTING CAGE GAMES

Players: 1 at a time
Area: Batting cage with mechanized pitcher
Equipment: Bat, helmet
Level of Difficulty: Easy–moderate

At one time or another, every Little Leaguer or softball player goes to a batting cage to work on his swing. There never seems to be enough time at a team practice to work on hitting to the degree that the individual players want, or need. A batting cage lets batters swing to their heart's content, or at least until their tokens run out. And they have the luxury of choosing the speed of the pitching they want to see.

Young people frequently go to a batting cage and just take cuts randomly, not working on strategy or placement. This is a mistake. All the great hitters are like philosophers in that they are motivated by ideas. Every great hitter strides to the plate with an idea in mind of what he wants to accomplish there, hoping to translate what he sees in his head into baseball reality. Now the pitcher may have a *better* idea and defeat the hitter, but if the hitter is smart he will file away what he has learned and when he faces that pitcher again, he may win out.

These same principles apply even when the pitcher is a machine. Don't just swing; go up there to accomplish something. Keep the stroke level, stride into the ball, and hit it. Hit it hard, and hit it somewhere. Now down the third base line, now up the middle, now to the right side. Imagine yourself in the tiny shoes of Wee Willie Keeler and hit 'em where they ain't.

A hitter can further challenge himself by limiting the number of swings at a given at-bat to ten. Ten swings to see what he can do. A pop-up is an out. A swing and a miss is an out. A weak dribbler to second is an out. But a grounder in the hole between short and third is a single. And a drive into the left-centerfield gap is extra bases.

At the end of ten swings, tally the results. Six out of ten? Not bad. Then step out and let the next person (Dad?) see what he can do. A game of this type helps players focus on hitting the ball hard rather than swinging mechanically at the unvarying, easily timed offerings of a mechanical pitcher.

STRIKEOUT

Players: 2 or 3
Area: Driveway, street, playground, yard
Equipment: Tennis ball, bat, baseball glove
Level of Difficulty: Moderate

Every ballplayer should know how to play this game by its name alone. Two players—pitcher and hitter—face off in baseball's primary struggle. A third person could shag balls in the outfield or perhaps act as umpire. Three strikes, and the batter is out. Pitcher moves to hitter, umpire to pitcher, and hitter to umpire.

The best backstop may be someone's garage door. There is no running. If the batter gets what is judged to be a fair and square base hit, the count starts over and he continues to hit. The pitcher must whiff him to get him out; no called third strikes. The hitter, however, cannot stand forever at the plate with his bat on his shoulder waiting for the perfect pitch.

CROSS THE STREET

Players: 2
Area: Street
Equipment: Tennis ball or soft baseball, baseball gloves
Level of Difficulty: Moderate

Cross the Street moves the game of catch out into the street. Watch out for cars, bikes, and other potential hazards. Using a tennis ball or soft baseball rather than a hardball, the players station themselves across the street from each other. The object of the game is to get the ball past the other. They may throw it really hard on the line, or toss a difficult fly, or bounce it sharply against the pavement like a grounder. To be sure, a tennis ball skidding across asphalt is as hard to catch as a garter snake. If the ball does get past, the person who threw it gets a point. Even if they cannot catch a ball, players learn very quickly the value of getting in front of a ball and using their body to knock it down.

BURNOUT

Players: 2
Area: Open space
Equipment: Baseball or
    softball, baseball
    gloves
Level of Difficulty:
    Moderate

Burnout is a game of catch gone to excess. One must think long and hard to determine what baseball skills Burnout teaches, although that does not stop youngsters from playing it.

In Burnout, one player tries to make the other player cry "Uncle!"—or words to that effect—because of the wind-scorching ferocity and power of the ball that he has just received in the pocket of his glove. Burnout should only be played in a large open space, away from windows. If there happen to be any people witnessing the spectacle, they should be well back. The ball frequently gets loose and goes rocketing places, despite the best intentions of the participants.

The two duelists stand a reasonable distance apart—not close enough to hurt anyone, but close enough to make a glove-popping impact. The arms of the contestants should be well-oiled before commencing a game of Burnout, for what they do is simply throw the ball as hard as they humanly can at each other. The ball has to arrive in a catchable spot; no headhunting allowed. The key is to snag the ball in the web; a direct hit to the pocket will sting. Even so, the victim will get his chance to be Doc Gooden and return the favor, with feeling.

One of the lingering myths of the Old West is that of the gunfight—two men meeting in a bravura showdown on the dusty main street of town. They draw, and one of them (invariably the bad guy) falls to the ground in a heap. The less glamorous reality was that most gunfights ended with both men walking away unharmed, often because their guns misfired or they purposefully shot into the sky or they were both such terrible shots they simply missed their target. Much the same thing occurs in Burnout. Most Burnout games do not last very long, usually only two or three throws apiece, and the two combatants—probably a couple of friends who just felt like having some fun—always walk away to throw again another day.

THREE FLIES—UP!

Players: 5–11
Area: Baseball field or
    street
Equipment: Baseball,
    softball, or tennis
    ball; bat, baseball
    gloves
Level of Difficulty:
    Moderate

In this classic game for both the street and the ballfield, one person hits fungo-type fly balls while everybody else fields. To win a turn at bat a player must catch three fly balls (or achieve 500 points). The fielders must all stay in the same general area; much of the fun of the game lies in the competition to see who can get to the balls first.

Oneupmanship or tomfoolery is not allowed. When a person says "I've got it!" she's got it and the rest of the players must back away to give her a fair chance. When there is a change of hitters, all the fielders lose their accumulated points and the scoring starts anew.

Obviously, a batter cannot always hit perfect fly balls, so a point system should be adopted to reward those players who cleanly field balls that bounce. A fly ball caught in the air counts for 100 points. A one-hop line drive counts for 75 points, if fielded cleanly. A two-hopper is 50 points, and three or more hop grounders are 25 points. In a version of Three Flies—Up! known as 500 Points, a fielder must reach 500 before taking a turn at bat. This system provides incentive for players to be aggressive and charge line drives.

The street version of Three Flies—Up! is played the same as the field game, with a few critical differences. Since the game takes place on a paved surface a hardball is inappropriate; use instead a softer ball such as a tennis ball. A tennis ball bounces like crazy and really flies off the bat, but it won't break anybody's windshield.

Playing with a tennis ball enables the players to add a wrinkle that doesn't exist in the field version of the game, for the simple reason that a ball won't roll on grass the way it does on asphalt. After making a catch, the fielder rolls the ball to the hitter and the hitter lays his bat on the ground. If the ball hits the bat and pops into the air, the hitter must catch it. If he snags it cleanly, no points are scored. But if the hitter fails to catch the ball after it pops into the air, the fielder who threw it receives a 100-point bonus.

ONE OLD CAT

Players: 3–12
Area: Baseball field or open area
Equipment: Baseball or softball bat, baseball gloves, 2 bases
Level of Difficulty: Moderate

One Old Cat is a simple game with a colorful name. The minimum number of players is three—pitcher, batter, and fielder. If there are more people about, they can take up positions in the outfield and infield, including catcher. The more fielders there are, the harder it is for a batter to accomplish his objective, which is running safely from home to first and back again after striking the ball.

Set the base up a fair distance from home plate. If sixty feet is too far, bring it in; if too short, move it out. The pitcher pitches, the hitter hits—and then it's off to the races! If there are only one or two fielders in the game, you might want to set aside an off-limits area—say, everything to the right of second base—and call it an out if anyone hits it there. After striking the ball the batter must run to first and then return home before the fielder can track the ball down and throw it back to the plate. If he succeeds, he gets another turn at bat; if he does not, out to the field he goes. If nobody is playing catcher, the pitcher covers the plate. The pitcher doesn't have to tag the runner (unless local rulemakers have decreed otherwise); tagging the base is sufficient for a put-out.

Few things in baseball are as exciting as the close play at the plate—the runner sprinting madly for home, the fielders relaying the ball sharply from one to another, the catcher tensing for the throw. One Old Cat duplicates that feeling.

INFIELD GAME

Players: 5
Area: Baseball infield
Equipment: Baseball, bat, baseball gloves, stopwatch (optional)
Level of Difficulty: Moderate

Taking infield is one of the most enduring of all baseball rituals. Infield Game adds some spice to it. A coach hits around the infield starting with the third baseman, allowing each position to field a grounder. However, if one of the players makes an error—a poor throw, a flubbed grounder—the coach starts the cycle over again with a grounder to third. A team—four infielders and a catcher—must complete an error-free circuit.

There are ways to make this game more difficult. Instead of just one grounder per infielder, make them field two or even three and throw without a miscue. If one has a really sharp group, add a clock to the proceedings. Time how long it takes for one group to do infield—including miscues and re-starts if there are any—and challenge other infield units on the team to do better.

RELAY THROW

Players: Unlimited
Area: Baseball outfield
Equipment: 2 baseballs
  or softballs,
  baseball gloves
Level of Difficulty:
  Moderate

One of the hardest things for a young outfielder to remember in the heat of a game—even major leaguers have trouble with it—is to throw to the relay person. "Hit the cut-off man!" is the refrain of Little League coaches everywhere who watch helplessly as their young charges, seeking to nail the runner rounding third with a Roberto Clemente-like laser beam to the plate, overthrow everybody and cause havoc for their team.

Relay Throw teaches young players to make faster and more accurate throws and to get into a good throwing position. Break the players into two groups of four or more and line the groups up parallel to each other down the field. The players on each team should be at an easy throwing distance from one another. As everyone gets the hang of the game, expand the distances to lengthen the throws. The teams should be close enough together that each team knows what the other is doing and whether they need to speed up their throws.

Start with the ball on the ground. At the coach's signal, the first player in each line scoops up the ball and throws to the next player. This player catches, pivots, and throws to the next player in line, who catches, pivots, and throws to the next person, and so on down the line. At the end of the line, the players reverse their throws. The winning team is the one that goes up and back first.

Granted, Relay Throw will not give young players the presence of mind to actually *make* those throws to the cut-off man during a game. But their coaches may take solace in the fact that they at least showed them how to do it.

BIG FLY

Players: Teams of 4
Area: Baseball field
Equipment: 1 baseball or
  softball per team,
  baseball gloves
Level of Difficulty:
  Moderate

Big Fly is another way to teach relay throws. There are four stations: outfield, cutoff man, relay person, and catcher. The game may start on the right side of the diamond, move to center, then left. It begins with a coach throwing a fly to the outfielder, who throws to the cutoff man, who hits the relay person, who pegs to the catcher at the plate. Each team scores points based on how well it performs these tasks.

Ten points equals perfection: The outfielder makes his catch, the other fielders make their catches, and all the tosses are on target. Drops or errant throws result in deductions. If the cutoff man drops the throw

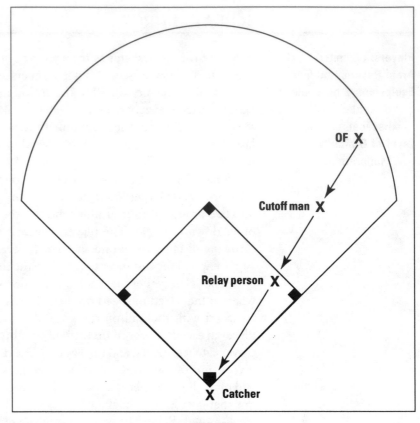

BIG FLY

from the outfielder, for example, but all the other exchanges are clean, the team scores 5 points. Two drops scores just 2 points, while poor throws should also be marked down two points. Judge accordingly. Each team rotates around the field, and the one with the most good throws and clean catches will emerge the winner.

BLOCK THE BALL

Players: 2–3
Area: Around home plate in baseball field
Equipment: Catcher's gear, baseballs or softballs
Level of Difficulty: Moderate

Let's not forget the catchers. As Casey Stengel said, "You have to have a catcher, because if you don't, you're likely to have a lot of passed balls."

Block the Ball will help prevent those balls from getting past the catcher. A coach stands between the mound and home plate and tosses ten to fifteen throws in the dirt. The catcher must get in front of these balls and knock them down with his body if necessary. For every ball in front of him that he blocks, he receives 1 point. For a ball on the side, 2 points. If there are two or more catchers on the team, match them in a down and dirty game of Block the Ball.

HOME RUN DERBY

Players: 2 or more
Area: Open area near fence
Equipment: Hitting tee, Wiffle Ball, Wiffle Bat
Level of Difficulty: Moderate

Home Run Derby lets junior sluggers swing for the fences. Set the game up against a fence—ideally, one that is six feet high or shorter. If the fence is short enough the outfielders get to be heroes too, climbing up to rob a hitter of a home run just like they do in the big leagues.

There is no pitcher; batters hit from a hitting tee. The tee should be about seventy-five feet from the fence. That constitutes a pretty good whack for a youngster swinging at a Wiffle Ball. Set the field up in a narrow inverted triangle shape so the person at the plate must hit the ball up the middle. Any balls hit outside the triangle are out. The batter gets only one swing. He does not run, but players still play the field waiting to catch any ball that lacks the propulsion to clear the fence. The fielders stand a safe distance away from the hitter, generally inside the triangle area.

Runs are scored only through home runs. A batter may get a base hit other than a home run, but all this does is keep the inning alive for his teammates. It does not figure in the scoring. There is no batting runners around in Home Run Derby; the bases are always empty when someone pastes a dinger. This simplified system is a boon for any coach or parent who must keep track of the runs scored.

Precise Hitting Contest

Players: 10 or more
Area: Baseball field
Equipment: Hitting tee,
  baseballs or
  softballs, bats,
  baseball gloves
Level of Difficulty:
  Moderate

This is a different sort of hitting test. Each player gets ten swings from a tee. Batters do not run, but players field. The batter scores points on where he or she hits the ball. A ball that gets through a gap in the infield scores 1 point. A ball between the outfielders counts for 2 points. A ball over the fence counts for 3. But a batter scores nothing on a ground-out, fly-out or an error. Players learn to hit to all fields and aim for the gaps. The batter with the most points earns a Coke after practice.

Work-ups

Players: 8–16
Area: Sandlot, baseball
  field
Equipment: Baseballs,
  bats, baseball
  gloves
Level of Difficulty:
  Moderate–advanced

Born of the sandlot, Work-ups is ideal for those times when there are not quite enough players available for a regulation baseball game. The name explains its object; players try to work their way up to the plate, where anybody worth his or her salt wants to be. Lots of hitting takes place, and yet players practice their throwing and fielding too.

The best Work-up games have every position filled, including catcher and all of the outfield. A minimum of four people form the hitting team. Nobody keeps score. The hitters try to register as many plate appearances as they can before making an out and taking their turn in the field.

Work-ups should resemble an actual game as closely as possible. With lob pitching, a batter should receive only three good pitches; if he cannot do something constructive with them he is out. Baseball rules apply. Batters hit and run, and the team on the field tries to get them out. A batter gets to stay on offense as long as he or she hits safely. After making an out the batter moves to right field, right field moves to center, center to left, left to short, short to third, third to second, second to first, first to pitcher, pitcher to catcher, and catcher—all right!—gets to hit.

Screen Ball

Players: Unlimited
Area: Baseball field with
  backstop
Equipment: Softball, bat,
  hitting tee
Level of Difficulty:
  Moderate

A typical backstop is divided into three segments—or four, counting the bottom, usually wooden section on the ground. These divisions provide the basis for one of the most popular of all hitting games, Screen Ball.

Set up the tee fifteen feet from the backstop, in an area between home plate and the pitcher's mound. Face the backstop. Each player gets one swing, then goes to the end of the line. He or she scores points

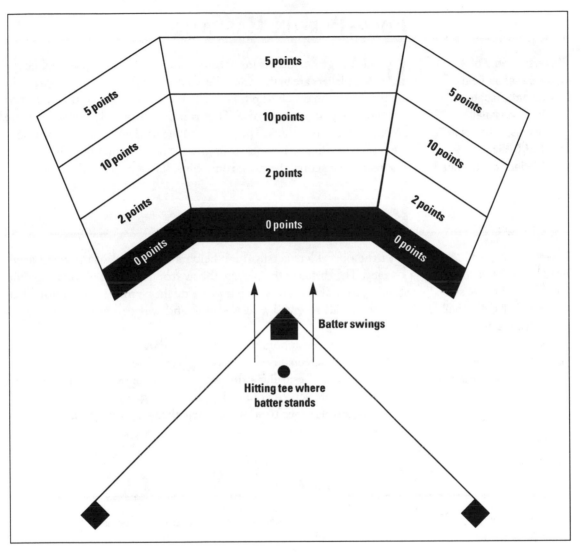

SCREEN BALL

according to where the ball lands on the screen. Players can only score points if they hit the screen; if the ball hits the lower wooden portion, that equals a ground-out and counts for nothing. The top third of the backstop counts for 5 points, a solid reward for a player who has lifted the ball into the air. The lower third of the screen is 2 points, a step above a ground ball. The richest reward comes when the player hits the middle segment of the backstop. Striking the middle portion equates to a line drive smash into center field, and scores 10 points for the batter.

FOUR-PERSON BASEBALL

Players: Teams of 4
Area: Baseball field
Equipment: Baseballs, bats, baseball gloves, 4 bases
Level of Difficulty: Moderate–advanced

Divide the group into teams of four. One team is at the plate, while the other players are in the field. Simulate game conditions using a pitching machine or a coach as pitcher. The batting team gets fifteen outs to see how many runs it can score. They run the bases and hit until they use up their allotment of outs. The players in the field, meanwhile, try to stop them from scoring. After one team hits, another team takes their place. The team that scores the most runs, wins.

BULLS-EYE!

Players: Unlimited
Area: Baseball field
Equipment: Softballs or baseballs, baseball gloves, screen of some kind
Level of Difficulty: Moderate–advanced

Pit the outfielders versus the infielders in this test of throwing accuracy. The distance the players throw from depends on their age and abilities; a good place to set up initially might be in the short outfield, as if a player had received a relay throw and was turning to cut down a runner at the plate.

Set up a screen at home plate. This could be a pitcher's screen or any of the various screens used by baseball teams to shield fielders during batting practice. Basically, a thrower must hit the screen to score. The lower half of the screen counts 3 points, the upper half 2 points. Ballplayers of any age love to show off their throwing arm. Bulls-eye! gives them a chance to do it.

OVER THE LINE

Players: Teams of 3
Area: Baseball field
Equipment: Baseballs or softballs, bat, baseball gloves, 3 bases
Level of Difficulty: Advanced

The contemporary game of Over the Line is fast, sophisticated and intense. Adult Over the Line leagues have sprung up around the country, most prominently in Southern California, because the game features lots of action sprinkled with entertaining bits of baseball strategy.

Three-person teams play Over the Line. The batter does not run, and he receives only two swings each time up. The batting team supplies the pitcher. The pitcher may pitch on his knees, very close to the batter, almost as if he was serving up lob balls to a small child just learning to hit.

The playing field has its own unique shape, a modified inverted triangle. At the tip of the triangle is home plate, from which the batter hits. He must hit the ball within the boundaries of the field—either the inverted triangle shape of the infield or the rectangular outfield. If he does

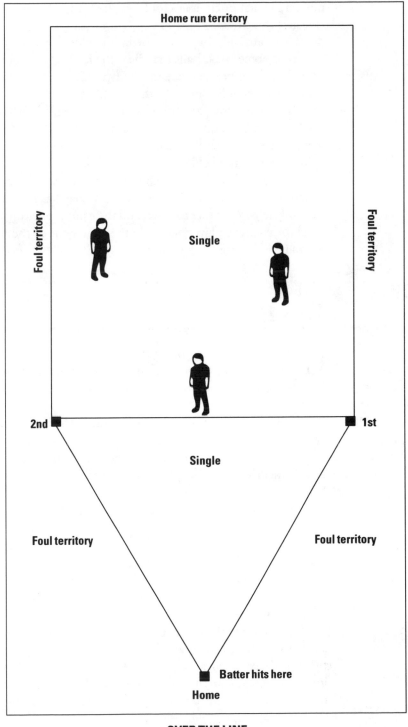

OVER THE LINE

not, on the first pitch, it is a foul. On the second pitch, it is an out. Each side gets three outs.

There are only two types of hits in this brand of Over the Line: singles or home runs. Balls that clear the farthest outfield line are home runs. The three fielders take up their positions depending on who is at the plate. Generally, one plays the infield and two patrol the outfield. As in the informal game, a ground ball fielded cleanly is an out. So, too, is a caught fly ball. Fielding errors count the same as a single. But the judgment calls of the sandlot game have been done away with, for all safe balls hit within the field of play are singles.

With only three bases (including home), it would seem to be much easier to knock people in. But the field of play has been narrowed considerably to compensate for that, and the game *is* exciting. It is especially good for younger players because the alignment of the field reinforces the value of hitting the ball up the middle.

GAP BALL

Players: 12–16
Area: Baseball infield
Equipment: Hitting tee, baseballs ("softies") or softballs, bats, 18 traffic cones
Level of Difficulty: Advanced

Games such as Screen Ball and Over the Line teach the value of driving the ball up the center of the field—not pulling it or swinging late. Gap Ball takes this fundamental principle of good hitting and builds on it.

In the infield, most base hits are found in the gaps between the fielders—between the first and second basemen, second and shortstop, and short and third. Set up the cones in these gaps. Imagine a normal infield arrangement with the fielders in place and put the cones where the infielders wouldn't be playing.

Set six cones at each station. The cones themselves have gaps between them. Each set of six is arranged in groups of three with a reasonably sized space in the middle. This is the 10-point gap, the spot the players will be aiming for. Ten-point gaps exist in the first base hole, over second base, and between shortstop and third. The players may hit left, right, or up the middle; wherever they aim, they will be trying to hit for the gaps in the infield.

In addition to the center gap, players may score if they hit into other, smaller gaps between cones. A hitter scores 2 points if he hits between the outside two cones in any set of three. If he hits between the two interior cones next to the big 10-point gap, he scores 5 points. So each set of cones contains (in order) gaps of: 2 points, 5 points, 10 points, 5

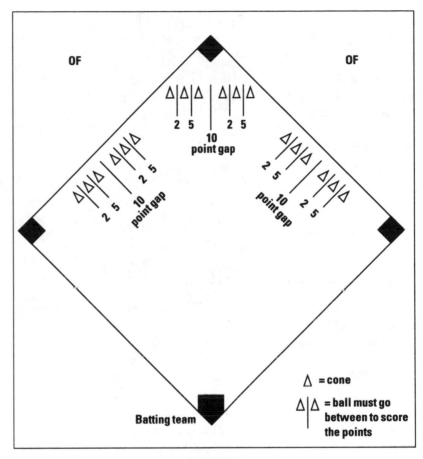

GAP BALL

points, 2 points. This arrangement allows a batter to score points though he may not hit the 10-point hole.

Gap Ball is complicated to explain but easily grasped once the cones are set up and the teams in place. One team of three or four players occupies each station. The players hit off a tee, getting two swings per at-bat. When the team at the plate makes three outs, each team moves one base over, with the team at first coming in to bat. Players in the field cannot interfere with a ball's movement, but they should of course scoop it up if it has gone astray or after it has passed through the cones. Any balls hit outside the cones are considered outs.

Teams can compete against each other or, better yet, all the teams can pool their scoring and compare their performance as a group from one day to the next. Yesterday we scored 87 points; today we broke 100!

BEAT THE BEEPER

Players: 11–20
Area: Baseball infield
Equipment: Baseballs or softballs, bats, stopwatch
Level of Difficulty: Advanced

One of the bad habits of young ballplayers is to watch the ball after they hit it instead of taking off for first base. Beat the Beeper will break them of this habit.

Playing Beat the Beeper requires a previous knowledge of how fast a player runs from home to first. When a batter makes contact with the ball, he takes off. If his best time to first is five seconds, the coach sets his watch just under that. The runner tries to beat his best time. When the time elapsed equals the pre-set time just under the batter's personal best, the coach sounds a buzzer or air horn, or just yells out. In this race against himself the batter will forget about the ball and zip down the line.

BASEBALL RELAY

Players: Unlimited
Area: Baseball field
Equipment: Baseballs, 5 traffic cones
Level of Difficulty: Advanced

Baseball players only have to run in short bursts. An outfielder may stand around doing virtually nothing for eight innings, then make an all-out sprint for a ball in the ninth inning that saves his team the game.

Baseball Relay is a conditioning exercise for young players. It can be done at the end of practice to give the team a good workout before it leaves the field. Divide the players into equal-sized teams and set out five cones in a straight line about ten to fifteen feet apart. When the whistle blows, the first person on each team runs a baseball to the first cone, sets it down next to it, and returns to the start. Then he takes a second ball and runs it to the second cone, returning again to the start. Then a third ball, etc. After he so carefully lays all the balls out, the second person in line on each team goes and picks them up, running up and back and up and back just as the first did. Then the third person lays the balls out, and the fourth person picks them up again. The constant movement of balls and bodies helps everyone forget about the running and focus instead on the fun and competition.

KILLER

Players: 8
Area: Baseball infield
Equipment: None
Level of Difficulty: Advanced

This is an aptly named conditioning game. Eight runners take up positions on the base paths—four on the bases, four halfway between each base. The coach blows the whistle, and off they go. Each person tries to catch the person in front of him. By the time one runner catches up with another, everybody will have run at full speed for ten to fifteen seconds. While these eight rest, bring on another eight. After the second group is finished, bring back the first group. This will whip the squad into shape *real* fast.

AROUND THE CIRCUIT

Players: Teams of 4
Area: Baseball infield
Equipment: Baseballs, bats, 4 bases, stopwatch
Level of Difficulty: Advanced

Around the Circuit is another conditioning contest, though not as tough as Killer. To simulate game conditions, a player faces a pitcher and hits from the batter's box. Where the batted ball goes is of no consequence; the players in the field simply shag it down. The hitter runs around the bases as if he were going for an inside-the-park home run. Each person's run is timed, and the team score is the cumulative time of the four persons on the team. Coaches should, of course, juggle the line-ups so that slower runners are grouped with faster ones. Around the Circuit helps players make a tight circle as they round the bases and concentrate on hitting each base with their foot in the right spot.

THREE

BASKETBALL

For some youngsters, basketball is not so much a game as a way of life. While their enthusiasm is admirable, they should realize that the method of play counts nearly as much as the hours they put in. If all they do every day is play pickup games or shoot around, they will never be as good as they could be.

Kareem Abdul Jabbar said once that the best thing that happened to him in basketball was the ban on dunking while he was in college. That forced him to develop other parts of his game, such as the hook shot and using the backboard, that he would not have learned if all he ever needed to do to score was jam the ball through the hoop. This is one of the virtues of playing games—different games, not just one-on-one or three-on-three. In basketball no less than other sports, games present different kinds of challenges in different ways, and by facing these challenges a young person improves and grows.

Shooting Around (Harvey Ball)

Players: 1
Area: Anywhere with a hoop
Equipment: Basketball
Level of Difficulty: Easy

Shooting Around is not a game per se; it's just shooting around. But there are games a young person can play when he is just shooting around with only himself as company. There is an old-time Jimmy Stewart movie in which he befriends a large, invisible rabbit named Harvey. Only Stewart can see Harvey, and he talks to him quite openly and sincerely. For these shoot-around games to work, a child needs to have the spirit of Jimmy Stewart and his friend Harvey in him.

A person can play Around the World or Horse by himself. First he shoots, then his invisible opponent shoots. His opponent should have a name. Pick one: say, Michael Jordan. That seems as good a name as any. So it's The Kid against Michael Jordan in a game of Around the World.

After they're done playing Around the World, The Kid might want to challenge Michael to a friendly game of One-on-One (page 62). Jordan is tough on D, but The Kid takes him inside and scores. As Jordan starts to sag a little, The Kid pulls up and bangs home a fifteen-foot J as the crowd roars its approval. A stadium full of roaring fans is essential to any game of "Harvey Ball."

So maybe now they move from One-on-One to a game of Five-on-Five, the real thing. His teammate feeds him a bounce pass and The Kid pulls up instantly, his high arcing rainmaker over Michael's outstretched hand drawing only net. But this Jordan fellow is nothing if not persistent, and even though he has just been embarrassed again on a give-and-go, he's staying with The Kid, hanging tough. Now the clock is winding down and everything is on the line. The crowd is really into it, just shaking the building down, and you can tell from the determined look in Jordan's eyes that he is simply not going to let The Kid beat him again. But The Kid has the ball, and he's backing Jordan down as the seconds keep melting away—6, 5, 4, 3 . . .

Suddenly The Kid turns. He goes up, Jordan goes up with him, he lets it go, and . . . and . . . and . . .

Yes!

HORSE

Players: 2 or more
Area: Basketball court, driveway hoop
Equipment: Basketball
Level of Difficulty: Easy

Horse is a classic basketball game, played by everyone who plays hoops. Both NBA stars and stars of the playground can get something out of it. It is a shooter's game. A player takes the ball to a spot of his or her own choosing and lets it fly. If the ball goes in, the other player must duplicate it. If he fails to do so, he gets an H. The ball returns to the original shooter and he shoots again. If this one goes in his opponent must again try to match it. A second failure gives him an O, and the ball returns once more to the original shooter who tries to put yet another letter next to his opponent's name.

But nobody makes everything, not even Michael Jordan. You can go to the bank on it: Eventually your opponent will miss, and when he does, it will be time to hang some letters on *him.* The loser is the person whose missed shots forces him to spell out H–O–R–S–E. If there are more than two players, the person with Horse goes out and the others continue on until a champion is crowned.

Other ways to play: There is an abbreviated version of Horse known as Out or, for some, Pig. Other spell out the word Poison. Same rules, just different letters.

Horse games can be made more challenging by attaching certain conditions to the shooting. Try different types of shots and require that the other players perform the shots in the same way. If a person sinks a bank shot, the next player must bounce the ball off the backboard as well; otherwise he or she gets a letter. Players may also want to perform a dribble and shoot sequence, a hook shot, or a running lay-up to practice more basketball skills than just the simple jumper. The rules should be agreed on ahead of time, however, to avoid disagreements later on.

AROUND THE WORLD

Players: 2 or more
Area: Basketball court, driveway hoop
Equipment: Basketball
Level of Difficulty: Easy

Around the World is another classic hoops game. As has happened with Horse, other sports have adopted variations of it. It, too, is a shooting game—the difference being that in Around the World the players must shoot from certain designated spots, rather than wherever they choose as in Horse.

Around the World begins at the base of the key (or lane), with a side shot from close in. If the shooter misses, it's someone else's turn. If he makes it, he moves to the next station halfway up the key. Make that one and move up again, this time to the corner of the free-throw line. From

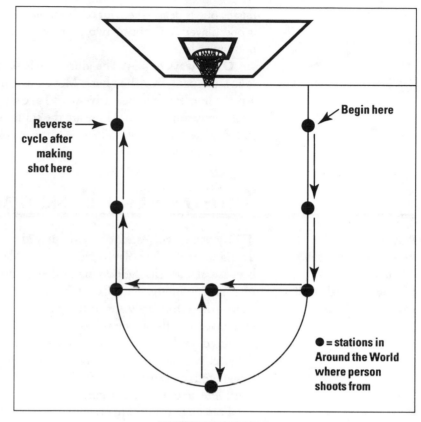

Reverse → cycle after making shot here

Begin here

● = stations in Around the World where person shoots from

AROUND THE WORLD

here, this is the shooter's travel itinerary: free-throw line, top of the key (where he or she gets two shots to make it), back to the free-throw line, then back down the opposite side of the lane. When he reaches that tricky little side shot at the bottom, he must make it twice—once to signify the completion of the circuit he has just been on, and once to start a new cycle. The person then goes back around the key again, making shots at all the various stations.

When a competitor misses a shot, he must remain at that station until he makes it. But there are second and even third chances in Around the World. If a player misses his shot he can call "Chance" and thus be granted a second try. (No Chance calls, however, are allowed on any of the bottom-of-the-key shots closest to the hoop.) But a Chance shot can backfire. A miss means that the player must forfeit all those hard-won shots he made earlier and retreat ingloriously back to the beginning of the cycle. Some Around the World players allow a "Life" shot following a missed Chance shot. A Life shot is a desperate gambit. A player who misses one is dead—i.e., out of the game. A Life shot is only worthwhile if one player is a shot or two away from winning and the others have nothing to lose.

Other ways to play: The journey around the world need not always follow the path described here. Move the game out and incorporate the 3-point line. Playing on a driveway? Take a piece of chalk and mark ten circles at various points. These are the stations that a shooter must travel to complete the circuit. When he buries his shot from the tenth designated circle, the game is over.

Two-One-Two Basketball

Players: 2 teams of 10
Area: Full basketball court
Equipment: Basketball
Level of Difficulty: Easy

Fifty years ago, American girls played what they called Half-Court Basketball. They played half-court while the boys played full-court because, it was felt, their young bodies could not tolerate so much running and jumping. Half-Court Basketball consisted of six girls on a team—three forwards and three guards. The forwards played offense and stayed strictly on one side of the floor; the guards played defense and remained on the other. The guards could not score, their job was solely defense. When they got the ball they threw it across the center line to the designated offensive players. Neither team's players could cross the mid-court line, keeping their running to a minimum.

Fortunately, girls are no longer restricted to a half-court game; they now play the same game as the boys, running and jumping and shooting with skill and verve. Still, Half-Court Basketball for young girls *and* boys has its merits. Nowadays, one version of it is known as Two-One-Two. The principles are the same as in the older game. The teams stay on one side of the floor exclusively, and nobody can cross center court.

Two-One-Two has the advantage of involving lots of players; twenty people can play at the same time. The game is essentially two five-on-five half-court games. If one defensive squad stops the offense from scoring, they toss the ball to their offensive teammates across the line, who face up against the defense on the other team. In this version the defenses play a two-one-two zone, hence the name. At halftime the offensive and defensive teams should switch roles, ensuring that all players get an equal chance to touch the ball.

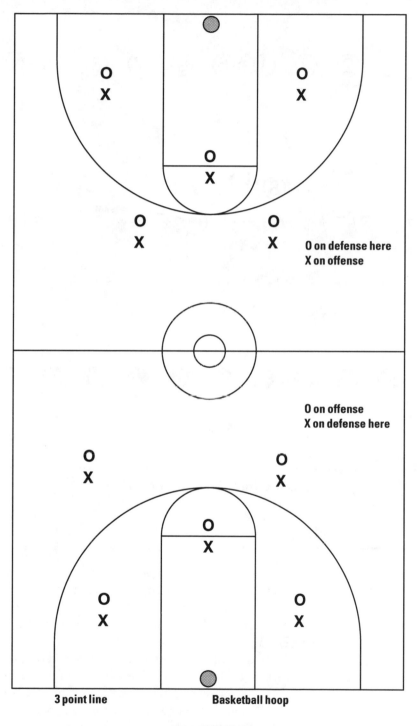

O on defense here
X on offense

O on offense
X on defense here

3 point line   Basketball hoop

TWO-ONE-TWO

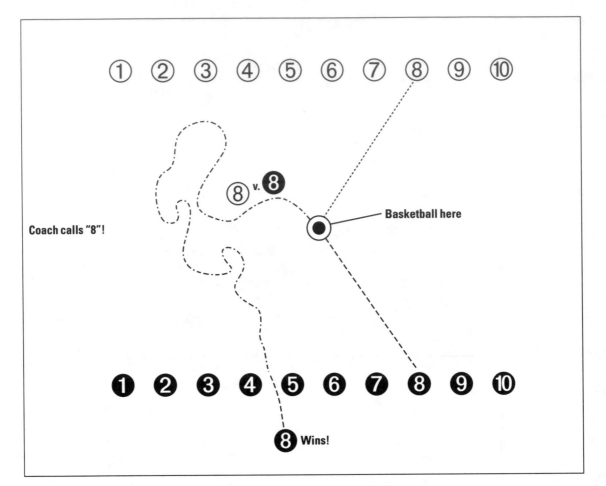

① ② ③ ④ ⑤ ⑥ ⑦ ⑧ ⑨ ⑩

⑧ v. ❽

Coach calls "8"!

Basketball here

❶ ❷ ❸ ❹ ❺ ❻ ❼ ❽ ❾ ❿

❽ **Wins!**

BASKETBALL STEAL THE BACON

BASKETBALL STEAL THE BACON

Players: Unlimited
Area: Basketball court
Equipment: Basketball
Level of Difficulty:
   Moderate

In the playground game Steal the Bacon, players line up in two lines facing one another with an object in the middle between them. One person from each line races up to the object in the center. Whoever gets there first grabs "the bacon" and tries to return to his line before the other person tags him.

In the basketball version of Steal the Bacon, the object in the center is a basketball. Each person in a line is assigned a number that matches the number of a person in the opposite line. When the teacher or coach calls out the number, the two race for the ball. But this is a basketball game, and so the person who gets there first must dribble the ball back into line while the other person guards him. Players learn to dribble under competitive pressure. The dribbler's team earns a point if he or she makes it back into line with the ball, while the defending player's team earns a point if the dribbler walks, carries, or loses the ball. Active vocal participation from the onlookers on both teams is a given. The team with the most points wins.

BASKETBALL STOP AND GO!

Players: Unlimited
Area: Full basketball court
Equipment: Basketball for each player
Level of Difficulty: Easy

This is a dribbling version of another old children's game, Red Light Green Light. Both basketball and soccer can play it. For a full explanation of the game, see Soccer Stop and Go, page 128. Stop and Go makes for excellent basketball dribbling practice. It teaches quick stops and starts, as the players must react instantly to the commands of the caller. In this basketball variation of the game, players can continue dribbling the ball after the caller says stop; they just cannot move forward. After one game of dribbling with the right hand, the players should switch over and use their left hand for the next one.

KNOCKOUT

Players: Unlimited
Area: Half basketball court
Equipment: Two basketballs
Level of Difficulty: Easy–moderate

The object of Knockout is to knock the person in front of you out of the game. The way this is done is by sinking a basket ahead of him. Knockout teaches concentration, hustling, and rebounding.

Have everyone line up behind the free-throw line. One person starts the game by shooting a free throw. If he makes it, he goes to the end of the line and remains in the game. If he misses, he has to quickly rebound the ball and lay it in. As he's doing this, the person behind him in line steps up and shoots a free throw. If *his* free throw goes in before the lay-up does, the person shooting the lay-up is out.

A good game of Knockout is a free-wheeling exercise that keeps everybody hopping. It is not necessary to make a free throw to knock someone out. Two people could have both missed their free throws and be shooting lay-ups. In that case, if the player who went second makes his follow-up lay-up ahead of the other, the first shooter is out of the game.

Other ways to play: A playground version of Knockout allows the players to throw at each other's ball. If a player misses his shot, he can quickly get the rebound and lay it back up as normal. Or he can stop his opponent from scoring in a most direct fashion by taking his ball and flinging it at the other person's. The one hard-and-fast rule of this version of Knockout is that players are allowed to throw their ball at the other person's ball at any time. The typical Knockout position is in front of the basket, ball poised in one hand as the free-throw shooter attempts his or her shot. If a person succeeds in knocking the ball off target, he can go and get his own ball, sink it, and throw it to the next person waiting in line, putting the onus on the poor fellow who's now running down *his* ball. This fellow must make *his* shot before the person at the free-throw line does. If he doesn't, he's out. But he can protect himself by knocking the other player's ball clean out of sight as well.

FREE-THROW SHOOTING CONTEST

Players: Unlimited
Area: Basketball hoop
Equipment: Basketball
Level of Difficulty:
   Moderate

Free-throw shooting contests have been the staple of amusement parks and country fairs for eons. Three shots for 50 cents. Make all three and win a stuffed animal. This is not as easy as it appears. Not even a 7.0-magnitude earthquake can shake the rims at most of these places.

A free-throw shooting contest is a way to motivate young players to practice this invaluable shot, and a way to raise money for the team as well. Open the contest to the public. Each contestant pays $2 to attempt fifteen shots. First prize wins $25, second prize $15, third prize $10. Post some signs around town and it is guaranteed that plenty of people will want to try their luck, just as they do at the county fair.

31

Players: Unlimited
Area: Basketball gym
Equipment: Basketballs
Level of Difficulty:
   Moderate

If the lay-up is the easiest shot in basketball, how come it is so easy to miss? Every basketball player who has ever played has experienced the humiliation of streaking down the court all alone, laying the ball up against the backboard, and watching helplessly as it trickles off the rim. A lay-up is like a three-foot putt in golf. You're supposed to make it, so it's no big deal when you do. But when you miss? Horrors, horrors!

For younger players, a lay-up is certainly no gimme shot; it is, in fact, very tough to hurl that big ball up there and get it through the basket. 31 gives them practice with their lay-ups and another tough basketball shot, the free throw.

Everybody lines up at the free-throw line. The first player in line begins by shooting a free throw. A made free throw counts 2 points; a miss nets nothing. After his or her shot the player rebounds the ball and heads for another basket in the gym to shoot a lay-up. Most gyms have several baskets hanging along the sides in addition to the two main ones; the contestants can use any one of these. A lay-up counts for 1 point. All the players must make their lay-ups before returning to the free-throw line, ensuring at least 1 point for each player every time he or she handles the ball. The first person to 31 wins.

If there's room, coaches can stage games of 31 at several different baskets at the same time, transforming the gym into a buzzing beehive of activity, with players shooting free throws, dribbling, and working on their lay-ups all at the same time.

Other ways to play: Make the game more difficult by asking players to dribble between shots with their left hand. Or turn 31 into a lay-up extravaganza: Forego the free throws and make the first shot a lay-up as well. Or forget about the lay-ups and make the second shot a jump shot.

DRIBBLING GAMES

Players: Unlimited
Area: Indoor basketball court or playground
Equipment: Basketballs, traffic cones (optional)
Level of Difficulty: Moderate

Dribbling is the fundamental skill of basketball. If a player cannot control the basketball, he will have trouble succeeding in the game. The two most common failings of young dribblers are their inability to use their left hand, and staring at the ball instead of looking ahead. Every dribbling game should teach young players to look up when dribbling and to feel comfortable using their left hand.

Dribbling relay races are a fun way to teach the skill. The competitors dribble down the floor with their right hand and back with their left. After this, give each player two balls and see how they do. Then let them try their luck with three or four balls. In the ensuing merriment, the players will be using their left hands without even noticing it.

The behind-the-back dribble and the through-the-legs dribble, while flashy, can serve a useful purpose for a playmaking guard trying to beat the press or shake a sticky defender. Set up a half-court race that tests those skills.

Obstacle races work well, too. Let the players weave through traffic cones set up around the court. Perhaps the first run is a simple speed test. But on the second run each person must dribble behind his back or through his legs as he goes around a cone.

CHASE THE DOG

Players: Unlimited
Area: Half basketball court
Equipment: 1 basketball per player
Level of Difficulty: Moderate–advanced

Chase the Dog is a terrific dribbling game, similar to King of the Dribblers (page 138) in soccer. Everybody has a ball and must stay within a defined area—say, half court to start. Anyone who goes outside the lines is out.

Each player rolls up a tee shirt and sticks it in the back of his or her shorts. It hangs from the shorts like a tail. Everyone tries to pull everyone else's tail while maintaining their dribble. When a dribbler loses his tail, he is out. As the number of dribblers decreases, so does the area of play—from half court to inside the 3-point line, to inside the lane. The clever dog who manages to hang onto his tail throughout the game, wins.

Other ways to play: Grab-Ass is Chase the Dog without the tails. It is advised for older players because there is closer, more physical contact. If a person loses his dribble, or his ball is knocked away, he is out. Gradually the dribbling area shrinks in size until only two or three players are left playing Grab-Ass in a small circle.

Or, taking a cue from the soccer game of Shark (page 138), release a player into the mix without a ball. He is the shark, and tries to bat away the balls of the dribblers. When a person's ball gets batted away, he becomes a shark too. The person who keeps his dribble and yet stays away from the Sharks, wins.

ONE-ON-ONE

Players: 2
Area: Driveway hoop, playground hoop
Equipment: Basketball
Level of Difficulty: Moderate

If a person gets tired of shooting around by himself and another player shows up, they might want to play a friendly game of One-on-One together. One-on-One is the primary building block of basketball. All other basketball games are extensions of it. The rules of One-on-One are simple: Put it in the hole and score points. After a miss, clear the ball away from the basket so there are no cheap scores. Blatant fouls should be called; generally, though, if a person's limbs are still attached to his or her body, the rule of the street is: Play it. The person who is fouled gets to take the ball out.

Scoring can be on a 2-point basis, playing to 22, or 1 point per basket playing to 12. Because achievement should be rewarded, the winner (or scorer) always takes it out.

Players can do some "schoolin' " in One-on-One, both giving and receiving lessons. The greatest lesson taught by One-on-One concerns size. Large people obviously have an advantage over small people in basketball. But One-on-One narrows the advantage. Smaller, quicker people can take the ball outside and score points from the perimeter. Unlike the Five-on-Five full-court version, the lane isn't clogged with bodies so a little person can slip past a big person and take it to the hoop without encountering heavy traffic. Also, a little person can outhustle those big lugs and get to loose balls faster. The only size that counts in One-on-One—perhaps in basketball in general—is the size of a player's heart.

21

Players: 2–3
Area: Half court
Equipment: Basketball
Level of Difficulty:
    Moderate–advanced

21 is a combination of Tip-in (page 65) and One-on-One. The game begins with a person shooting free throws and the other person (or persons) acting as rebounder. The free throw made on the first shot counts for 2 points; after that they're 1 point apiece. The shooter shoots until he misses.

When the shooter misses the fun begins, because after a miss the ball is in play, and a one-on-one (or two-against-one) game commences. Players can also score by tipping the ball in; that earns them 2 points and a trip to the free-throw line. One ruthless version of the game stipulates that tipping the ball in after a missed free throw automatically sends the person who shot the ball back to zero. That person has been "tipped out."

Following a missed free throw, 21 is essentially a one-on-one game. Players must clear the ball after rebounding an opponent's shot. A person cannot simply take a ball down and put it back up quickly and expect to score points that way. When a person scores a basket, he receives 2 points. This brings the one-on-one play to a stop, and the scorer goes to the free-throw line to shoot. The other players stand in places along the key waiting for the next miss.

As in Tip-in, the winner must hit 21 on the button—no 22s allowed. If someone goes over 21 he must go back to 12. Much of the fun of 21 occurs in the strategic battles that take place late in the game when a player with 19 points who does not trust his free-throw shooting slams the ball hard against the backboard in order to catch his opponent napping. This way, he can get an easy rebound and pick up his final 2 points by scoring a basket. But his opponent should be wise to such stratagems, and be ready to respond accordingly.

10

Players: 2 teams of 3 or more

Area: Half basketball court

Equipment: 2 basketballs

Level of Difficulty: Moderate–advanced

1 0 is a team-shooting game. Players divide into teams of three, and the team that shoots the best earns bragging rights over the other.

The game can start from anywhere on the court—free-throw line, baseline, behind the 3-point line—and go anywhere. Each jump shot that goes in counts for 1 point. The shooter rebounds, and passes back to his or her teammate, who shoots from the same spot. After each member takes his or her turn, the contest moves to another spot. Though the game is only to 10, each individual puts up a surprising number of shots in a friendly competitive atmosphere.

SHOOT-OUT

Players: 2 or more shooters, 1 rebounder

Area: Basketball court, driveway hoop

Equipment: Basketball, stopwatch (optional)

Level of Difficulty: Moderate–advanced

For its annual All Star weekend, the NBA stages a "long distance shoot-out" which pits the best 3-point shooters in the league against one another in a timed competition. This is a variation of that game, more suited to the still-developing skills of the NBA stars of the future.

Shoot-out is a great game for a parent and child to play together. The parent acts as rebounder and timekeeper, while the child works on his outside shooting with the clock adding an element of pressure.

For high school or older players, all shots should take place beyond the 3-point line. But the 3-point shot is way too far for younger kids, so they should stay generally around the paint. The shots should be far enough away to be a challenge, but not so far that it discourages any hope for success. It's best to start close to the basket and gradually move outward as the shooter's prowess increases.

The shooter shoots from five different stations placed in a semicircle around the hoop—beginning at the baseline area on the right side, moving up toward the top of the key, and back down to the baseline area on the other side. The stations should not just be on one side of the basket; part of the challenge of Shoot-out is making the shots from different areas on the court. The shooter travels around the court, shooting from different angles and thus getting different "looks" at the basket, as the TV commentators like to say.

Shoot-out is an uptempo game. Players cannot stand around and size up their shots forever; it's bombs away! After the shooter shoots—miss or make—he moves to the next station. Each time he makes it, he gets 1 point. Or a player can get three shots per station. He gets 3 points if he makes it on his first try, 2 points on his second, and 1 point on his third. If he misses all three, he still must move to the next station. The person with the most points at the end of a complete circuit—all five stations, and back again—is the winner.

More advanced players can try this game under the pressure of a clock. Give the player a reasonable period of time—five minutes, three minutes, one minute—to complete the circuit. Use the same point system, but now the shooter must negotiate his way around the hoop while having to worry about running out of time. The player who can learn to ignore the clock while concentrating on his shooting will be a winner in this game, and in basketball itself.

Tip-in

Players: 2–3
Area: Half basketball court
Equipment: Basketball
Level of Difficulty: Advanced

Tip-in is a deceptively hard game that combines free-throw shooting with the agility and coordination needed to tip a ball in midair back into the basket.

The object of the game is to get to 21. Free throws count for 1 point, while a tip-in counts for 2. Only a person's first free throw—if he makes it on his first try—counts for 2 points. The winner must hit 21 on the nose. If a player goes over 21, he must return to 12 and try again. This requirement means that players must use strategy, perhaps even deliberately missing a free throw to make sure they don't exceed 21.

One player begins as the free-throw shooter, while the other stands at the hoop ready to react to a missed shot. If the shooter keeps making his free throws, he or she keeps scoring points and there is nothing the other player can do (except, perhaps, make noises to throw the shooter's timing off). But he'd better not get caught flat-footed, because the only way he can get out of the rebounding position and onto the free-throw line is to tip the ball in. Tipping requires timing and agility. When the ball comes off the rim or backboard, a person must bat it back into the basket with his fingers as he is jumping. Timing is crucial, for a player almost always must be at the apex of his jump for a tip to be successful.

If the tip does not go in, the player on the line continues shooting. But if the rebounder makes the tip—Yes!—he becomes the free-throw shooter and his opponent moves down to the low post to try his hand at this most delicate of basketball arts.

25

Players: Unlimited
Area: Full basketball court
Equipment: 1 basketball per team
Level of Difficulty: Advanced

25 works on passing and lay-up skills, and builds conditioning. Two players throw chest passes back and forth as they run down the court. They maintain the same distance between them—about the width of the lane—all the way. When they reach the end of the court one of them shoots a lay-up. Then they turn around and do it again. The goal is to go twenty-five times up and down the court without missing a lay-up. If they miss, they must return to zero and start over. 25 builds strong bodies.

Obviously, 25 is too tough for young players. A much less taxing game of 2 or 4 may be more appropriate. It may also be that the punitive element of 25—starting over on a miss of a lay-up—is too harsh for some. Eliminate this and institute a team-scoring system in its place. For each lay-up they make, they score 2 points. For each successful passing run they make, they earn 1 point. So if a team does everything right on a single trip down the floor, it scores 3 points. The first team to 15 wins.

CUTTHROAT

Players: 6–15
Area: Half basketball court
Equipment: Basketball
Level of Difficulty: Advanced

Cutthroat is three-on-three basketball. One team of three plays another team of three, while other teams of three wait off court under the basket ready to jump in when the 1-point game on the floor concludes. There is no slack time in Cutthroat; after one team scores, the next trio jumps in. A team plays until it loses.

If younger players have one universal bad habit, it is that they tend to dribble the ball too long. For junior versions of Cutthroat, a one-dribble-per possession rule may be wise. One dribble and pass, one dribble and pass. Youngsters will learn to move without the ball. After one team misses a shot and the other rebounds, clear the ball to the top of the key or the 3-point line.

Other ways to play: Four-on-four Cutthroat, or two-on-two; even five-on-five. Teams rotate in quickly after each point.

Three-Man War

Players: 3
Area: Basketball court
Equipment: Basketball
Level of Difficulty:
  Advanced

This game comes with a caveat. As its name suggests, Three-Man War can get a little rough, and the players *can* get banged up. But that may be why so many young people enjoy playing it.

Three people play at a time. Match up the competitors by size. A very tall or very big person will have an obvious advantage over a smaller player, because the game takes place entirely in the paint. Fouls should be called only if they are flagrant. This is basketball at its most Darwinian level; only the strong survive. The competitors must stay inside the key. If the ball bounces away, designated rebounders stationed around the floor retrieve it and throw it back inside. Inside the paint, this is a two-against-one game, making the guy with the ball a marked man.

Three-Man War is a rebounding drill, an inside shot drill, and a shooting-with-a-guy-hanging-on-you drill. The first person to score three hoops wins.

Three-on-Three Fast Break

Players: Unlimited
Area: Full court
Equipment: Basketballs
Level of Difficulty:
  Advanced

Three-on-Three Fast Break simulates gamelike fast-break situations for both offense and defense. Two groups of players line up on each side of the court at about the half-court line. These two groups compete against each other.

The game begins with three players with the ball. They start at their end and come roaring down the court, confronting two defensive players from the opposite team. The offensive squad initially has a three-on-two advantage and it is their job to exploit it. If they work well and fast, they should put the ball up and score.

If they tarry, however, they will lose their advantage because a defensive player enters the game after the offensive team passes half court. This fast-moving third defensive player will even up the numbers and eliminate the offensive advantage. The two teams play straight-up three-on-three until a score or the defense captures the ball.

The trailing defensive player cannot simply enter the court wherever he wants. He runs along the half-court line, touches the floor at the center jump circle, and then runs into the fray. This approximates how a trailing defensive player would enter a fast-break situation—not suddenly from the sides, but down the center area of the court.

Three-on-Three Fast Break flows seamlessly. The offensive trio goes off the floor, retiring to their line on one side of the street. The three

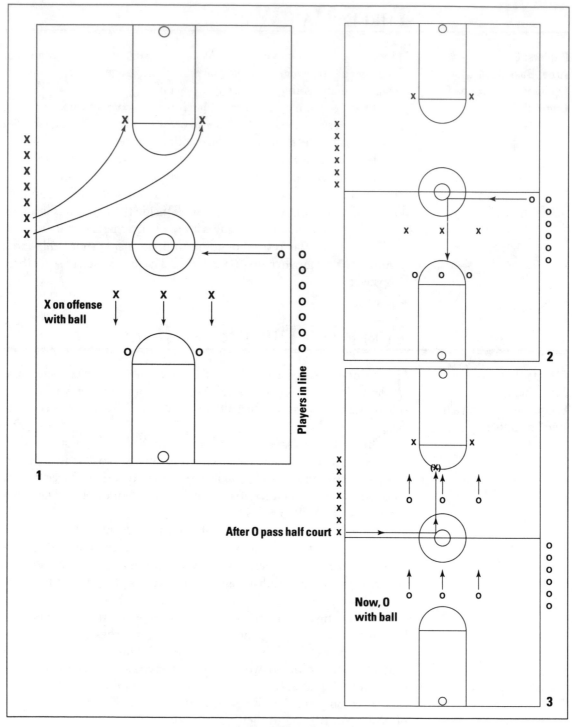

**X on offense
with ball**

Players in line

After O pass half court

**Now, O
with ball**

1

2

3

THREE-ON-THREE FAST BREAK

defensive players switch to offense, picking up the ball and bolting down the court in a fast break of their own. Waiting for them, of course, are two new defensive players who have filled in from *their* line. The two lines alternate feeding players onto the floor, with each line always filling to the same basket. Every player naturally plays both offense and defense.

The game moves so quickly that keeping track of all the scoring for both teams will be difficult. But by game's end most players will probably be worn out from all the running, and not care.

FOUR

BILLIARDS (POOL)

Pool, or pocket billiards as it is more formally known, is a terrific indoor activity for older children and teenagers. Shooting pool requires concentration and an ability to think ahead—valuable traits for anyone to have.

A billiards table fits nicely into a garage or rumpus room. Invite the neighbors over, and rack 'em up. If that's not possible, many boys' and girls' clubs and community recreation centers in this country have tables. They have found that billiards is a highly social game that appeals to children looking for an alternative to traditional after-school activities.

LAG FOR BREAK

Players: 2 or more
Area: Billiards table
Equipment: Cue sticks, cue ball
Level of Difficulty: Easy

Lagging for break is technically not a game; it is what pool players do prior to a game to determine who breaks. But it has all the ingredients of a game. It requires skill and touch and it is fun, especially when one player lags his ball a whisker's length farther than his buddy's.

Set the cue ball up behind the "head string," the invisible line where players break from. (The "foot spot" at the other end of the table is

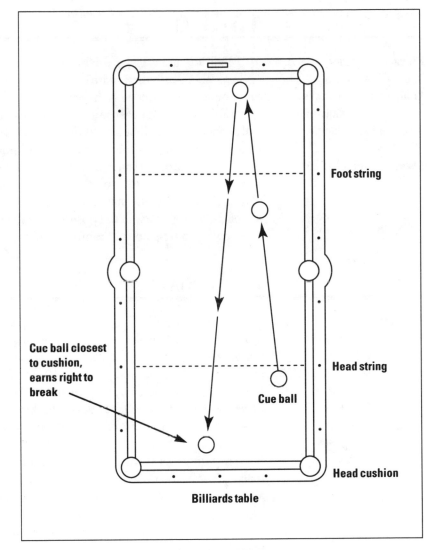

Foot string

**Cue ball closest
to cushion,
earns right to
break**

Head string

Cue ball

Head cushion

Billiards table

LAG FOR BREAK

where balls are spotted and where they rack the balls to start a game.)
Bank the cue ball off the far or foot cushion, sending it back the opposite
way toward the head cushion. The ball cannot touch the head cushion; if
it does, the player automatically loses. Though he will certainly be
tempted, a player cannot blow on a stalled ball to keep it rolling. Nor can
he suddenly jerk his opponent's ball away, stab it with his cue, or otherwise impede its progress if it appears to be embarked on a better lag than
his own. The person whose ball rolls closest to the head cushion without
touching it earns the right to break.

15-Ball

Players: 2 or more
Area: Billiards table
Equipment: Cue sticks, 15 object balls plus cue ball, triangle rack
Level of Difficulty: Easy

15-Ball is a great game for beginners or immediate players (it also helps them with their math). Players do not call their shots and they can shoot at any object balls they choose. The higher-numbered balls are preferable, however, because a player scores the number of points of the ball he shoots down. If he shoots down the 15-ball, for instance, he scores 15 points. If he shoots the 14, he scores 14 points. And so on.

The winner of the game is the person who scores the most points. In a two-person game, 61 points mathematically eliminates the losing player. Befitting its title status in this game, the 15-ball is placed at the top of the triangle rack in the position usually occupied by the 1. All the other balls can be placed in random order.

Cutthroat

Players: 3 or 5
Area: Billiards table
Equipment: Cue sticks, 15 object balls plus cue ball, triangle rack
Level of Difficulty: Easy–moderate

Cutthroat is a great group game. Three people is the ideal number of players, but five also works. Essentially the game works like this: Shoot the other person's balls. The person who breaks gets the balls numbered 1–5, the second player 6–10, and the third player 11–15. In a five-player game, the groupings are in variables of three: 1–3 for the first player, 4–6 for the second, 7–9 for the third, 10–12 for the fourth, and 13–15 for the fifth. A person plays as long as at least one of his assigned balls is on the table.

The winner of Cutthroat is the person who has at least one of his balls remaining on the table when all the others have been sunk. Players alternate turns, trying to shoot one another's balls. Shooting down all of an opponent's balls forces him to leave the game. It is possible, however, to return from the dead in Cutthroat. If one player scratches the cue ball, the other two players get to bring up a ball of theirs that has been sunk. A person who has been put out of the game can get back into it this way. Given new life, this player resumes his normal turn and can come back to win the game if he is able.

8-Ball

Players: 2
Area: Billiards table
Equipment: Cue sticks, 15 object balls plus cue ball, triangle rack
Level of Difficulty: Moderate

One of the most popular of all billiards games is 8-Ball, perhaps because the rules are so simple. One player shoots the balls numbered 1 to 7. The other player shoots the striped balls from 9 to 15. After someone successfully pockets all of his balls, he aims for the 8. If he shoots it in—after calling his pocket, of course—he wins.

Whether a person shoots stripes or solids is determined by the first ball made. If the first person who makes a ball sinks the 11, for instance, he shoots stripes. If a player sinks the 8-ball before he has run his allotment of balls, or if he shoots the 8 into any pocket other than the one he has designated, he loses. Some players deem the 8 a neutral ball that can be used as the first ball in combination shots; others do not. (A combination is defined as "a shot in which the cue ball first strikes a ball other than the one to be pocketed, with the ball initially contacted in turn striking one or more other balls in an effort to score.") It is generally acceptable to use the 8 as the second ball in a combination, as long as it doesn't go in. If a person sinks the 8 on the break, the players can do one of two things: declare this lucky soul the instant winner, or call this act a fluke of nature and rack the balls again.

One must always strike one's own balls—whether stripe or solid—first. Using the other person's balls as the second ball in a three-ball combination is allowed, though seldom successful. Accidentally sinking the cue ball is called a scratch. If a player scratches, he must spot one of his balls. Some 8-Ball partisans believe that having the stripes gives them an advantage because the stripes are flashier and easier to see than the solids. This is superstition more than anything else. The fact is, if a person cannot shoot pool, there is no hiding this fact no matter what balls he is aiming for.

9-Ball

Players: 2
Area: Billiards table
Equipment: Cue sticks, 9 object balls (1–9) plus cue ball, triangle rack
Level of Difficulty: Moderate–advanced

9-Ball is a game of classic simplicity and beauty, starting with its rack. A 9-ball rack is diamond-shaped, with the 1-ball at the forward point of the diamond and the 9-ball nestled in the center guarded by the other balls.

There are only nine numbered balls in 9-Ball, compared with the fifteen in 8-Ball. In 8-Ball, once a player's designation (either stripes or solids) is established, he can shoot his balls in any order he wishes, depending on where they lie on the table. Such is not the case with this

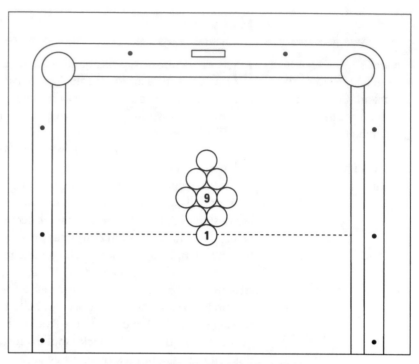

9-BALL RACK (DIAMOND-SHAPED)

more skillful game. 9-Ball is a rotation game. Players must always strike the lowest-numbered ball on the table first, though the balls do not have to go in in order.

There is a divine cruelty to 9-Ball. One learns about life in 9-Ball, and the lessons it teaches are not easy to accept. A player can go on a hot streak and run eight straight balls. But if he does not sink the 9-ball, he loses the game. Many younger players like 9-Ball because, with fewer balls on the table, they can make an impressive impact on the break.

ONE-POCKET

Players: 2
Area: Billiards table
Equipment: 15 object balls plus cue ball, triangle rack
Level of Difficulty: Advanced

One-Pocket is an unusual game because a player can score only by hitting balls into a certain pocket. All the other pockets on the table are essentially off limits to him. Prior to the break, each player chooses one of the corner pockets at either end of the table. If one player chooses a corner pocket at the foot end of the table, the other player must choose a pocket at the opposite or head end of the table. These pockets remain each player's respective target pockets for the game.

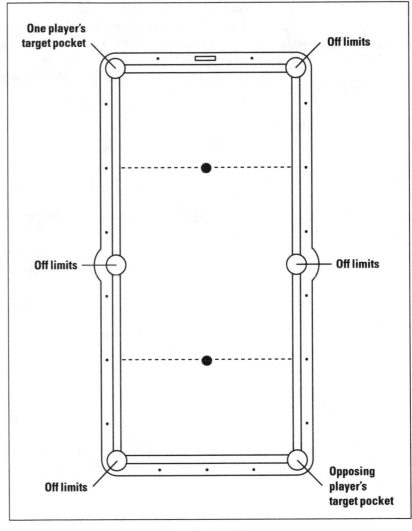

One player's
target pocket

Off limits

Off limits

Off limits

Off limits

Opposing
player's
target pocket

ONE-POCKET

The winner is the person who scores eight balls in his target pocket. The object balls do not count for their numerical value in this game; the contest is over who can shoot a majority of balls (out of fifteen) into his target pocket.

If a person knocks a ball into any pocket that is not a target pocket (that is, neither his nor his opponent's), it is considered the equivalent of a scratch and the ball is spotted back on the table. (As is customary, a scratch of the cue ball nullifies any ball that is made on that shot.) If a person happens to shoot a ball into his opponent's target pocket—well, that's the shooter's tough luck. The ball stays down and counts to his opponent's total. And if the shooter knocks the ball into his opponent's target pocket that gives his opponent the magic number of eight, the shooter has sealed his doom and lost the game.

FIVE

BOWLING

Some people argue that bowling is merely recreation, not a sport. In fact, many of these same people say a similar thing about golf—that it is more of a pastime or a hobby than a sport. Word-splitting arguments of this kind do not matter to children, who just want to have fun, and they should hardly matter to their parents. Bowling requires concentration, touch and physical coordination. Like billiards, it is a social game that attracts youngsters who may or may not be particularly athletic. The young can play with the old and an entire family can play together. Now how many sports can claim that?

CARPET BOWLING

Players: 1 (plus understanding parents)
Area: Hallway
Equipment: Bowling ball, pillows
Level of Difficulty: Easy

The teaching of games, like the teaching of reading or any important activity, always begins at home. Children can begin bowling at four or five years of age. Easily intimidated by the bright lights and noisy clatter of the bowling lanes, in the beginning they can practice in the comfort of their home.

Any house or apartment has the makings of a bowling alley. A *carpeted* hallway is advisable, of course, especially if there are people living below. The rule in carpet bowling is: the lighter the better. (The lightest ball available to a youngster is six pounds.) The possibility exists that, despite the best efforts of the laneskeepers, a ball will go astray. A lighter ball will not stop this from occurring, but it may lessen the damage if it does.

Remove all obstacles from the area—also, any antique heirlooms or precious family treasures. At the end of the hallway, place a pillow or two. The pillow acts as backstop and should prevent the creation of any unsightly holes in the wall. Pins (or a home substitute) are not necessary; aiming for the pillow alone is trick enough for the young kegler.

Parents should adopt a generous view toward Carpet Bowling. If a lamp falls over or the plaster on the walls gets chipped, they should simply see these events as a byproduct of growing up, much like the pencil marks on the door jamb that measure the stages in a child's growth. In future years, parents may indeed proudly point to that gouge in the hallway and say, "Oh yes, that's where Ellen threw the bowling ball when she was six."

SCOTCH DOUBLES

Players: Teams of 2
Area: Bowling lanes
Equipment: Bowling ball
Level of Difficulty: Easy

One way to keep a child's attention from straying too far in the typically long bowling game is to pair him with someone else in a game. In Scotch Doubles, the players alternate throws—one person throws the first ball, the next person throws the second ball. Their score derives from the combined efforts of each. Scotch Doubles makes for spirited family games, teaming parents with children or the children versus their parents.

NO-TAP

Players: Unlimited
Area: Bowling lanes
Equipment: Bowling ball
Level of Difficulty:
    Easy–moderate

When a bowler gets "tapped," it means that he or she has been left one pin short of a strike. Nine pins have obediently fallen, but one solitary rascal has stubbornly refused to yield. No-Tap turns every bowler's aggravation into a game.

Nine pins count as a strike in No-Tap. If all ten pins happen to go down, that is all well and good. But a No-Tap strike of nine pins counts as much as a ten-pin strike. If a person knocks down nine and leaves one, his turn is over and the pins are reset just as if he has thrown a normal strike. A person only throws for a spare when more than one pin is standing—and again, he or she receives credit for the spare if nine pins go down. A No-Tap 300 is when someone throws twelve nine-ball strikes.

SNAKE BITE

Players: Unlimited
Area: Bowling lanes
Equipment: Bowling ball
Level of Difficulty:
    Moderate

Even worse than being "tapped" is being "snake-bit." That is when a bowler gets a split, leaving, in the worst possible scenario, the 7- and 10-pin standing. Picking up these two pins on the second roll requires the razzle-dazzle of Merlin the Magician.

Snake Bite, like No-Tap, turns a conventional aggravation into a game. Bowlers go the opposite of their usual desires and try to get a split; taking it out afterward is not required. Scoring may be handled in the conventional way, with bonus points for actually handling the splits, or the winner can be the person who rolled the most splits over the course of a game. (Illustration is on next page.)

UNDER THE SHEETS

Players: Unlimited
Area: Bowling lanes
Equipment: Bowling ball,
    bedsheets
Level of Difficulty:
    Moderate

It's highly unlikely that a family would play Under the Sheets on an ordinary evening out at the bowling lanes; it's more of a camp or bowling league activity. Still, if there's ever an opportunity to play it, it's great fun.

Under the Sheets is bowling blind. Hang some bedsheets across at least two bowling lanes at the foul line. They should hang down far enough so that the bowlers can see neither the guide marks of the lanes nor the pins. Relying on memory, or instinct, the bowlers must simply let the ball go. The scorer, of course, charts what happens to the pins. This is a good game for any child who is trying to guide the ball—a common failing of all ages of bowlers. It is also highly entertaining to watch the kids roll and then quickly peek between or under the sheets to see where their ball went.

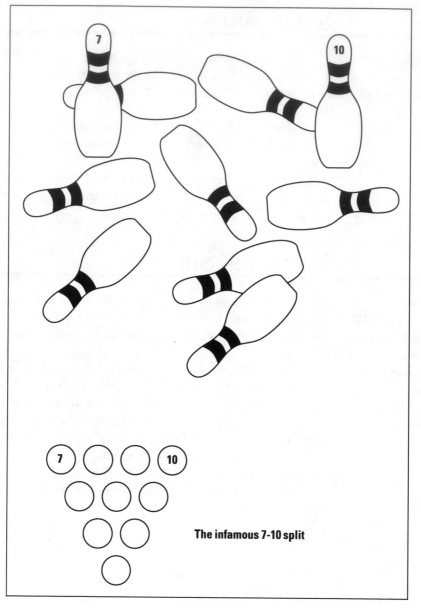

The infamous 7-10 split

SNAKE BITE

FIELD HOCKEY

Field hockey is primarily a club or school sport played in parts of the East and Midwest. Although it is not one of the mainstream sports, there is much about it to recommend to young people. It is a freewheeling game that calls upon many of the same skills used by its wintertime cousin, ice hockey.

It is no wonder that anthropologists believe that cave people played a primitive version of field hockey. Boiled down to its primary elements, it basically consists of hitting a ball with a stick. Of course, there have been some refinements since the days of the Neanderthals. Players can only hit the ball with the rounded side of the stick, not the flat part, and they can only touch the ball with the flat of their hand, no other part of the body. The object of the game is to put the ball in the goal and score.

OBSTACLE DRIBBLE

Players: Unlimited
Area: Playing field or gym
Equipment: Field hockey sticks, balls, traffic cones
Level of Difficulty: Easy

Obstacle races are one of the simplest ways to let children have fun and build skills in sports. Basketball, football, soccer, golf, and field hockey are just a few of the sports in which young players can improve their agility and footwork by running obstacle courses.

Obstacle Dribble allows field hockey players to work on their dribbling while learning to keep control of the ball. Divide the group into teams. Each team must negotiate a series of obstacles—traffic cones are probably the most common—laid out on the field so as to encourage quick stops and starts and runs. Players weave in and around the cones with the ball always in tow. They hand off to the next person in line, who takes his spin around the cones. The team that goes up and back first wins.

FIVE IN A ROW

Players: Unlimited
Area: Playing field or gym
Equipment: Field hockey sticks, balls
Level of Difficulty: Easy–moderate

Five in a Row is a passing game. There is more to field hockey than just scoring goals, and Five in a Row instills this lesson. There is no goal in the game, which allows the players to concentrate on improving their team play by spreading the ball around to their teammates.

The way a team scores points is by passing. A team scores 1 point by passing the ball among themselves five consecutive times. The opposing team tries to stop them. If they steal the ball, they try to pass five times and score a point themselves. Dribbling is permitted, but frowned upon. The team that earns 3 points first wins the game.

HIT AND STOP

Players: Unlimited
Area: Portions of playing field
Equipment: Field hockey sticks, balls
Level of Difficulty: Easy–moderate

Hit and Stop is a great way to work on hitting and fielding. The game begins with two lines of players standing opposite one another. A player is paired with the person opposite him in the other line. At the coach's whistle, each duo begins hitting back and forth. One pass equals 1 point. The team that has accumulated the most points at the end of a minute wins. As the skills of the players grow, the two lines can be moved farther and farther apart.

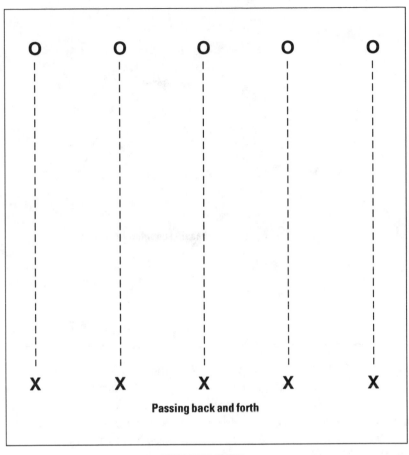

Passing back and forth

HIT AND STOP

Triangles

Players: Unlimited
Area: Portion of playing field
Equipment: Field hockey sticks, balls
Level of Difficulty: Moderate

Triangles is another hitting-and-fielding game, but with more potential variations than Hit and Stop. Arranging the players in the form of a triangle gives them more freedom and flexibility. Rather than simply hitting the ball back and forth they can vary their choices.

Divide the players into groups of three. Each person should be ten to fifteen yards away from the other two. For the first time around the triangle, the players must pass the ball in a clockwise direction. For the second go-around, it's counter-clockwise. If a competitive element is desired, the teams can compete to see how many times they can pass the ball around the triangle in a minute.

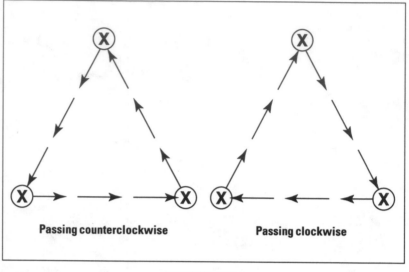

TRIANGLES

MONKEY IN THE MIDDLE

Players: 3 or more
Area: Portion of playing field
Equipment: Field hockey sticks, balls
Level of Difficulty: Moderate

Monkey in the Middle is essentially a game of keepaway. Two players control the ball, hitting it back and forth between them, while a third player, the "monkey," tries to whisk it away from them. If he succeeds, the person who hit the ball last becomes the monkey and a new game commences. Younger players may require boundaries so the monkey has a better chance of coming up with the ball.

Monkey in the Middle need not be restricted to three players. With a larger group, there can be two or three monkeys chasing the ball with five or six players in control of it.

Bully

Players: Unlimited

Area: Portion of playing field

Equipment: Field hockey sticks, balls

Level of Difficulty: Moderate

Bully is reminiscent of the playground game Steal the Bacon (and the basketball version of Steal the Bacon, explained on page 58). Two groups of players line up parallel with each other about fifteen yards apart. Each player has a number that corresponds to someone in the opposite line. The ball is placed in the middle between the two lines. When the coach calls out a number, the two players with that number face off against each other to control the ball. The player who gains possession tries to bring it back to her line, while the other player attempts to stop her, steal the ball, and return it to her line. The player who succeeds in bringing the ball back to her line scores a point for her team.

SEVEN

FOOTBALL

Football is a lot of fun. It's fun to throw and run and catch and kick and defend. It's also fun to watch. Just as they play youth soccer, baseball, and basketball, ten- and eleven-year-olds in many parts of the country play organized youth football. They put on the pads, strap up the helmet, and block and tackle and hit.

For obvious reasons, though, youth football must be well supervised. Both parents and coaches need to watch their young Montanas and Paytons with a close and careful eye. Football is a rough sport—at any age—and the safety and well-being of the players obviously supersedes all other considerations.

There is, of course, an alternative to tackle football. Flag football and touch football possess many of the joys of the game with fewer risks. The mostly noncontact games in this chapter are suitable for both flag and tackle ball.

BALL-AWARENESS GAMES

Players: Unlimited
Area: Football field
Equipment: Footballs
Level of Difficulty: Easy

A football is not like other balls. It is not round like a baseball, nor does it bounce like a basketball. It has pointy ends and is subject to the strangest bounces. Youngsters who want to play with this most unpredictable of balls should get to know it first.

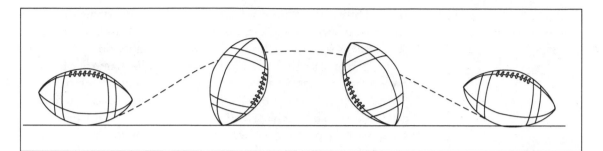

BALL-AWARENESS GAMES

Every player can play these ball-awareness games, linemen included. It is heartbreaking for a young person with his heart set on playing receiver and catching the ball to learn that he has to become an interior lineman on his youth football team because he is too big or weighs too much. These games give youngsters like that an opportunity to touch the ball, even if only during practice.

Break the group into two or more teams. At the coach's whistle, the players pass the football backward over their heads down the line. The first team to move the ball up and down the line wins. Next, everybody squats in the center's position and passes the ball through their legs. When the ball reaches the end of the line, everybody turns around and sends it back the other way. Next try simple handoffs, or laterals.

It is easy to add a conditioning element to these games. Make them continuous. Once a player makes the handoff, he runs to the front of the line: Hand off, run to the front, hand off, run to the front, etc. In this way the teams move down the field. The first team to the end zone wins. These games improve physical conditioning, build team spirit and togetherness, and let everyone get in on the fun of handling a football.

THROW IT!

Players: 3–4 on a side
Area: Park or football field
Equipment: Rubber football
Level of Difficulty: Easy

Throw It! is a simple pass-and-catch game that's excellent for small, encumbered spaces. Seven or eight youngsters can play it even though several assorted nonplayers—a family picnicking on the grass, a woman reading a book against a tree, a man and a woman lolling romantically together on a blanket—may impinge on parts of the field. If such obstructions clutter the field of play, use a small rubber football. Then if the ball gets away and bonks somebody, people won't be as upset.

The two sides stand about ten or so yards apart, directly facing one another. Throw It! is a loose, informal game. The sides do not have to be even; there can be four players in one group and three in the other. Nobody keeps score, and the sides are not in competition.

One person with the ball starts by calling out the name of a person in the other group. That person becomes the receiver and tries to get open to receive the pass. The others on his side swarm around him in an attempt to stop it. The receiver receives, the defenders defend, the thrower throws. After the pass, the receiver—whether he caught the ball or not—becomes the thrower and calls out the name of someone in the opposite line. He can never call the name of the person who just threw to him, thus ensuring that everybody gets to throw and catch in turn. The thrower must release the ball within a count of five, and the receivers cannot run up too close to the person with the ball. If someone intercepts a throw, he becomes quarterback and the game continues.

Obstacle Races

Players: Unlimited
Area: Football field
Equipment: Traffic cones, car tires, hula hoops, blocking pads
Level of Difficulty: Easy–moderate

Obstacle races are a challenging, yet fun, way to prepare for football games, where running backs really do have to dart and dip and dodge to avoid obstacles on the field, some of which are bodies lying on the ground. But there is no reason why running backs alone should participate. Backs can compete against backs, linebackers against linebackers, linemen against linemen. All positions and levels of players can improve their agility and coordination through these games, competing either individually or on teams.

An obstacle course can consist of whatever materials are at hand, plus imagination. The players can high-step through car tires on the ground or through hula hoops. They can weave among traffic cones, making sudden cuts and stops. They can tumble on the grass, run cross-legged, hop on one foot, spring backward, even run a few stadium steps. They can hurtle blocking pads or some other obstruction like so many steeplechase runners.

In the soccer game of Cow Patties (page 130), the participants run through a designated area littered with dozens of balls. Anyone who brushes against a ball takes a position on his knees as a "cow patty" and tries to tag other players coming through on the next wave. Whoever they touch joins them as a cow patty and helps with the tagging. This is another type of obstacle game perfect for running backs. In every football obstacle game the runners should always carry a ball, of course.

DEFENDER

Players: 3
Area: Park, football field, street
Equipment: Football
Level of Difficulty: Moderate

Defender helps promote three skills essential to football: passing, receiving, and pass defending. The game consists of a quarterback, a receiver, and a defensive back, with the defender trying to spoil the offensive designs of the other two.

This is a touch game. The quarterback and receiver can advance only by completing passes. They get four downs per series, just as in regular football, but they must complete three passes to make a first down. If they do this, they can remain in their respective roles, driving down "the field" toward the goal line. If it happens that their first two passes fall incomplete and they have no hope of obtaining a first down, they must drop all pretense and go for the bomb.

After a touchdown or if a quarterback-receiver duo fails to get a first down, a change of positions takes place. The quarterback moves to receiver, the receiver to defender, and the defender to QB   and the game starts over going the opposite way. If the defender intercepts a pass, he automatically goes to quarterback and the quarterback becomes defender.

THE PASSING GAME

Players: 2 teams of 6–8 or more
Area: Football field
Equipment: Football, flags
Level of Difficulty: Moderate

Passing a football intimidates a lot of youngsters because they feel they don't do it very well or they look funny when they do it. The Passing Game can help erase those inhibitions and make even the meekest of children into a Slingin' Sammy Baugh. The rules are the same as in regular football, but there is one strategic difference: The offense can pass anywhere, anytime, in any direction.

One team kicks off to start the game. A player on the receiving team can pass backward to a teammate, who can pass forward to another teammate, who can pass sideways, and on and on until the person with the ball gets his flag pulled. The same holds true for a play from scrimmage. The normal prohibitions against forward laterals or passing from beyond the line of scrimmage do not apply. Once somebody crosses the line of scrimmage he can still throw downfield to an open teammate, who, in turn, can himself throw downfield—the ultimate object being to make it into the end zone.

The Passing Game gets everybody involved. And as the players run around, excitedly throwing the ball back and forth, one or two might even wonder: "So what *was* the big deal about passing a football anyway?"

21

Players: 2
Area: Portion of football field
Equipment: Football
Level of Difficulty: Moderate

21 is an accuracy game for throwing the football. Two players stand ten to fifteen yards apart and throw the ball back and forth. A throw to the other person's chest area counts for 2 points. That's where the quarterback should put it. A throw that is a catchable ball but forces the receiver to extend his arms scores 1 point. A throw below the waist or beyond arm's reach that forces the receiver to move his feet counts for nothing. The first person to 21 wins. If a person passes 21, he must return to 12.

CENTER SNAP GAME

Players: 2
Area: Portion of football field
Equipment: Football
Level of Difficulty: Moderate

Center Snap Game is an example of how to take a routine football act—in this case, hiking the ball to the punter—and turn it into a game. Follow the same principle as in 21: 2 points for a hike straight into the punter's hands, 1 point if he reaches or bends. A center can work on his hike in a shotgun offense, too.

DISTANCE THROW

Players: Unlimited
Area: Football field
Equipment: Football, traffic cone
Level of Difficulty: Moderate

Distance Throw is a classic test for quarterbacks, but every player on the team may want to get in on it. Line the players up at the forty-yard line, and see how far downfield they can throw the ball. Accuracy is important; the ball must land between the hash marks in order to count. The longest throw should be marked with a traffic cone, giving the others a goal to shoot for. If someone throws a ball beyond that point, mark it accordingly and then let the players try to surpass it.

MORE QUARTERBACK GAMES

Players: 5–7
Area: Football field
Equipment: Footballs, targets of various kinds
Level of Difficulty: Moderate–advanced

Beyond sheer distance, a quarterback must throw with accuracy. One of the simplest ways to test a quarterback's arm is through target practice. The classic football test employs a car tire or some other target hanging from a fence. The throwers can be awarded points for how well they do: 10 points for a clean throw through the doughnut, 5 points if it hits the rubber and goes in, 2 points for just hitting it. The game can be restricted to quarterbacks, or all the players can enter a team contest.

A more elaborate target game establishes five stationary targets on a field—left, right, middle, deep left, deep right. Targets could be traffic cones, blocking pads, or even receivers standing at the different spots. Give each contestant five tries and see how many they hit. But no just standing and firing; they must drop back and throw.

A tougher challenge is known as Read and Recognition. This time, the targets—receivers on the team—move. Instead of the quarterback picking the receiver, as is usually the case, one of the receivers calls out. The quarterback must respond instantly and hit him with a pass.

Quarterbacks can benefit from obstacle games as well. The quarterback weaves through cones or other obstacles and when he reaches the line of scrimmage, he hits an open receiver.

TIP GAME

Players: 4–5
Area: Portion of football field
Equipment: Football
Level of Difficulty: Moderate–advanced

Tip Game helps teach defensive backs how to catch a tipped pass—something every secondary player should know how to do. Four or five people can play this game—passer, receiver (usually the coach), and two or three defensive backs. The quarterback and receiver have supporting roles; the defensive backs are the focus of this contest.

The quarterback throws a pass to the receiver. But instead of catching it, the receiver purposefully tips it behind him in the area of the three backs, who must react to the ball and try to snag it in the air. The first one who catches three balls moves to quarterback, quarterback moves to receiver, receiver joins the defenders, and the game begins anew.

FLAG FOOTBALL

Players: 2 teams of 8
Area: Football field
Equipment: Football, flags
Level of Difficulty: Advanced

Flag football is an excellent compromise between the unstructured game of touch and the rigors of tackle. There is obviously not as much contact as in tackle, and by using flags coaches and teachers will not have to arbitrate disputes such as this:

"You didn't touch me!"

"Yes I did!"

"Prove it!"

"I don't have to prove it. *I touched you!*"

"Liar!"

"Takes one to know one." Etc., etc.

Flag football has its own set of rules distinct from tackle. A regulation team consists of eight members, five of which must be stationed on the line. The interior offensive linemen must get down in a three-point stance, although the defense can stand any way they want. A fumble can only occur on a kickoff; if a ball gets loose, then it is live until controlled. In the ordinary course of play, however, a team cannot lose the ball to the other team by fumbling it.

The genius of flag football (apart from that ultimate arbiter, the flag itself) is in the arrangement of the playing field. There are three hash marks spaced twenty yards apart on an eighty-yard field. The offense gets four downs to travel to the next hash mark, wherever that may be. It does not matter if the hash mark is an inch away or nineteen yards away; if it goes past the line, the offense gets four new downs. This arrangement minimizes the role of referees. Whereas in tackle football, with first downs every ten yards, a bevy of officials and their helpers is needed to make the measurements, spot the ball, and operate the chains—none of this is required in flag football.

Touchdowns are the standard 6 points. Conversions may be figured two ways: Setting the ball seven yards out from the goal will net the offense 2 points if it makes it in; five yards out equals 1 point. Or, award 2 points for a pass conversion and 1 point for a run. Of the two approaches, the former may be the superior because it retains the drama of the offense hatching a play in the huddle that will put them across the goal line, with the unknowing defense reacting on the spot to stop them.

The flag itself, which can be made of nothing more elaborate than a torn bedsheet, must be twelve inches long. A Flag cannot be stuck so deep into the trousers that a stranger would need a court permit to remove it. They should be placed to the side at the waist and allowed to dangle loosely. Nor can a runner with a ball jump, hurdle, spin, straight-arm, or otherwise guard his flag. The flags must be reachable for all, and when a defender grabs one cleanly and brandishes it in the air, the play is dead.

SEVEN-ON-SEVEN

Players: 14
Area: Football field
Equipment: Football
Level of Difficulty:
    Advanced

This universal football game pits seven defensive backs against an offensive team of seven—quarterback, center, and five receivers. The game helps the defense work on its pass coverage. The defensive backs learn to be aggressive and go after the ball. The offense should show various "looks"—backs split out, two tight ends, shotgun—to confuse the defense. The quarterback must throw the ball on a count of four or five, to give the defense a fair shot. In high school the defense might have to run a lap if it gives up a completed pass, while the offense runs the lap

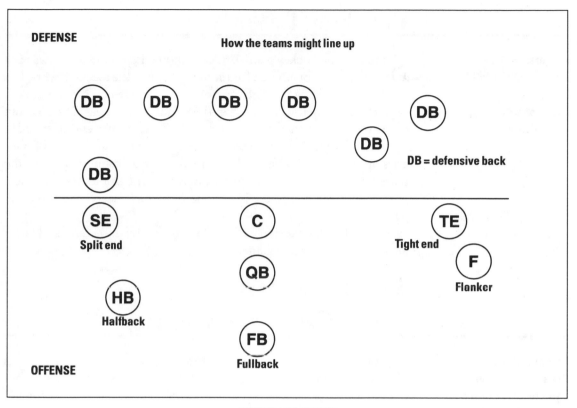

DEFENSE

How the teams might line up

DB = defensive back

Split end

Tight end

Flanker

Halfback

Fullback

OFFENSE

SEVEN-ON-SEVEN

if the defense deflects or intercepts. This may be a bit too stern for younger players. For every completed pass the offense wins 2 points; for every deflection, the defense wins 1 point. Interceptions count for 2 points. The first team to 15 (or 21) watches the other run a lap or do push-ups.

Tackle football teams primarily use Seven-on-Seven, but it will work in flag too. Because flag requires fewer players, just make it a six-on-six game.

First and Goal

Players: 10–14
Area: Football field
Equipment: Football
Level of Difficulty:
Advanced

Another universal game on the order of Seven-on-Seven. It can be run with interior linemen or not. Set the ball inside the ten-yard line. The offense has four downs to get it in. Like all games, mixing it up now and again—letting a lineman play running back—will keep the players loose and the practice lively.

POM POM TACKOWAY

Players: Unlimited
Area: Football field
Equipment: None
Level of Difficulty:
    Advanced

Similar to the hockey game British Bulldog, Pom Pom Tackoway is a rough game, not advised for the very young or the meek of heart. It is essentially a tackling game. Everybody starts at one end of the field except for the tackler, who stands in the middle of the field. The sole aim of the runners is to make it to the goal line at the other end of the field without being tackled. The sole aim of the tackler is to stop them. Boundaries are necessary, because the runners can't be running all over the place. Once a person gets tackled, he becomes a tackler too. The tacklers grow in number until there is but one runner left, who is declared the winner.

A touch or flag version of Pom Pom Tackoway is a gentler and faster alternative to the tackle game.

TACKLE THE BALL
(A.K.A. CREAM THE CARRIER)

Players: Unlimited
Area: Football field
Equipment: Football
Level of Difficulty:
    Advanced

Tackle the Ball is not so much a football game as a free-for-all. It is more of an endurance test than a game. It can get very physical, but nobody wears pads. Indeed, as one former Tackle the Ball aficionado says, looking back on his days playing the game in junior high, "I'm surprised no one broke anything."

There are no teams in Tackle the Ball, although temporary mini-alliances form over the course of a typical match. These alliances usually consist of ten or so smaller guys ganging up on one large fellow who, since he is carrying the ball and making headway toward the goal line, must be brought down. One person can't do it alone, so everybody piles on until the big lummox is dragged to earth. Once he is down, he must surrender the ball to whoever can grab it. That person takes off running until he, too, gets tackled and coughs up the ball. Some misguided individuals may try to hang onto the ball after they are tackled, thus causing pile-ups of body-crushing proportions.

As in ordinary football, reaching the end zone is the goal of the person carrying the ball. But unlike ordinary football, a ball carrier can run to whichever end zone he chooses. Even if only within steps of one zone, he may suddenly reverse field and run ninety yards back the other way if he wishes. He may do this as a means of escaping his pursuers, although, of course, there is no escaping the mob for long in Tackle the Ball.

If a person crosses the goal line with the ball in his possession, he scores a point. It is not unusual for entire games to occur without anyone ever crossing the goal line. Except by group consent, there are no time-outs in Tackle the Ball. As many people as are willing can play, and a typical game lasts about as long as lunch recess. The biggest and toughest guys often dominate, although fast, crafty guys can do all right too.

Tackle the Ball veterans also advise that anyone who wears glasses should either get contacts or find another form of recreation; glasses do not tend to have a high survival rate in this game.

GOLF

One should always take the long view in teaching or learning golf. It should be thought of as a lifetime activity. Teaching a youngster to play golf is like planting a sapling. It won't look like much in the early years, but over time, if given the proper care and nourishment, it will ripen and mature into glorious, full-leafed adulthood.

Maturity is essential to good golf. The hard reality is that many nine- and ten-year-olds do not have the strength to wield a golf club properly and must wait until their middle teen years before they can. Young players should work on their posture and positioning, learn basic swing patterns, and be encouraged to think about the kind of shot they want to hit before they hit it, rather than simply stepping up to the ball and giving it a good lick.

Golf will have plenty of time to frustrate and challenge these youngsters as their skills and physical abilities grow. While they are young, let them have fun. The primary building blocks of an early golf education should be joy and a love for the playing. If a child loves what she is doing, she is more likely to spend the time it takes to play the game well. But, lacking this foundation, her budding interest may dry up and blow away.

21

Players: 2–4
Area: Backyard or putting green
Equipment: Putters, balls, tees
Level of Difficulty: Easy

There are almost as many putting games in golf as there are betting games, but it is important to realize that a putting game does not have to take place on a putting green. A game such as 21 can work equally well in the backyard, assuming Dad has mowed the lawn recently.

In this case, a "hole" is two wooden tees laid flat on the ground about five inches apart. The holes on this backyard course may be arranged to suit the fancy. They can be set up like a putting green, with as many holes as the players want. The players should follow the course, moving from the designated first hole to the second, third, fourth, and so on. When a person shoots the ball through the tees on his first stroke—

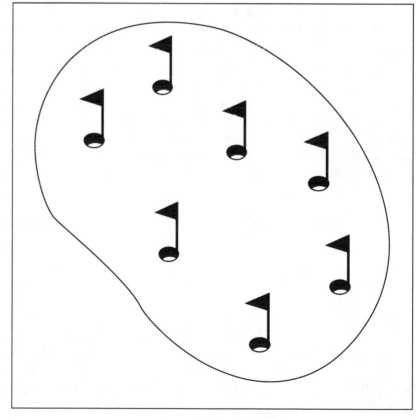

21, 7-11, AND TWO-PUTT PAR

the equivalent of sinking the putt—he scores 2 points. If the ball grazes a tee before it goes through, score 1 point. Balls made on the second stroke only count for 1 point. The two players move around the course and the first one to score 21 wins. As is customary in 21 games, going over that magic number returns the player to 12, where he or she must start accumulating points again.

7–11

Players: 2–4
Area: Backyard or putting green
Equipment: Putters, balls
Level of Difficulty: Easy

A shorter, slightly different version of 21. In this game, the shot closest to the hole (or tee) counts for 1 point, while sinking the putt earns 2. The winner is first to 11. If a player goes over 11, he or she returns to 7.

TARGET GOLF

Players: 1 or more
Area: Backyard or open area with fence
Equipment: Targets, golf clubs, Wiffle Balls or golf balls
Level of Difficulty: Easy–moderate

Golf is essentially a target-shooting game, so why not set up actual targets? Rip up old sheets and paint bulls-eyes on them, or make bulls-eyes out of sturdy cardboard. If playing with Wiffle Balls, post the targets along a fence in the backyard or another suitable area. Swing one-handed—first with the right hand, then the left—then with both hands. Then go back to single-handed. See how many times a player can hit the targets in a row.

BUCKET BALL

Players: 1 or more
Area: Backyard or open area
Equipment: Buckets lined with foam, chipping wedge, Wiffle Balls or golf balls
Level of Difficulty: Easy–moderate

Bucket Ball allows chipping practice. Play it in the backyard with Wiffle Balls or, if possible, set up the game around a putting green or warm-up area at the golf course and use real balls. Tilt the buckets—plastic kitchen trash cans could work—slightly toward the golfer, who stands about ten feet away. (Move back in increments of five feet as the player's expertise allows.) The buckets should contain foam padding to prevent the balls from bouncing out. A player scores 3 points for a clean chip into the can, 2 points for hitting the rim and bouncing in, and 1 point for simply hitting the bucket.

TWO-PUTT PAR

Players: 2–4
Area: Putting green
Equipment: Putters, balls
Level of Difficulty:
  Easy–moderate

Every hole in this putting contest is a par 2, so if a person rolls it into the cup on his first stroke, he goes 1 under. Two strokes on the hole equals par of course, but three putts earns a dreaded bogey. The total number of strokes over eighteen holes, or the number of holes won, will determine the winner.

DANGEROUS

Players: 2–4
Area: Teeing ground
Equipment: Golf clubs, 1
  ball apiece
Level of Difficulty:
  Easy–moderate

Dangerous, or Poison as it is also known, is the game to play while waiting around on the tee at the start of a hole. Players should use the club and ball they are going to tee off with on that hole.

Normally there are two sets of tees—blue and red—at the start of a hole. Sometimes there are also white, or championship, tees. Each player should set up at one blue tee and, taking turns, try to stroke their ball against the other blue tee. Once someone hits it, he becomes "dangerous" and can start knocking the other players out of the game. The way you knock someone out of the game is to hit his ball with your ball. If there are four players in the game, the person whose ball is remaining after the others have been knocked out wins the hole.

Some players play that a person must also hit the red tees before becoming dangerous, but that is more a function of time than anything else. If the foursome in front of you are duffers, there may be time to play the blue, red, *and* white tees. Some also say that a person cannot hit any of the tees after he becomes dangerous; if he accidentally hits a tee with his ball he's out, much like scratching on the 8 in 8-Ball Billiards.

Dangerous requires strategic thinking. It may be that all four players are dangerous and each can knock the other out of the game. So if one dangerous player misses while shooting for another, he can easily get thumped out of the game if his ball does not roll far enough away. If you must miss, miss long. This forces the other players into a similar strategic dilemma, and the one who gives in—who misses close—almost invariably loses the hole.

Dangerous can be dangerous in more ways than one. If it is one of those awful dog-day afternoons when nothing is going right, the game being played on the tee may turn out to be more fun than what is happening elsewhere on the course.

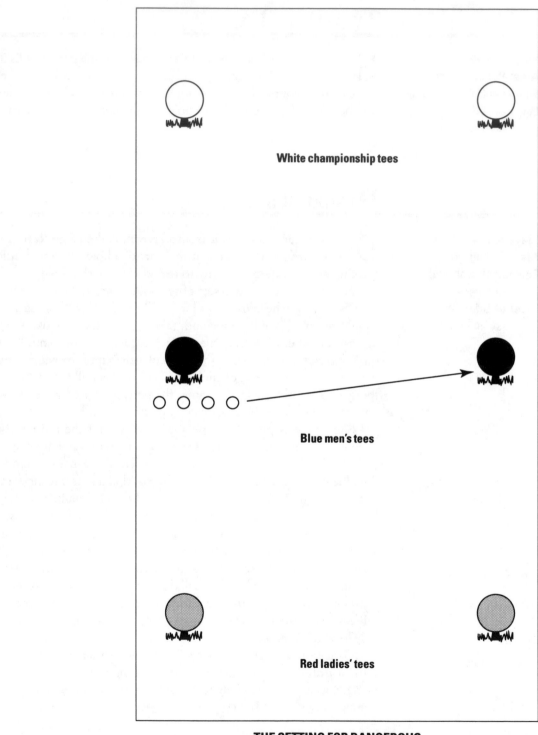

White championship tees

Blue men's tees

Red ladies' tees

THE SETTING FOR DANGEROUS

LONGEST-DRIVE CONTEST

Players: Unlimited
Area: Driving range or
golf course
Equipment: Driver, balls
Level of Difficulty:
Moderate–advanced

A Longest-Drive Contest is like a home run hitting contest in baseball. Sooner or later, a person who plays the game is going to want to see how far he can hit the ball. Golf can sometimes seem too much like work, especially when pounding away on a driving range, and a chance to really crank it up and lay into one is a way to break up the monotony.

A Longest-Drive Contest should not be just a test of length, but of accuracy as well. The ball must travel basically straight, between two pre-established markers, in order to count. Long and wild does not figure, only long and under control. If out on the course, the ball must stay in the fairway, and the losers buy the winner a Coke.

CLOSEST TO THE PIN

Players: 2–4
Area: Golf course,
putting or chipping
green
Equipment: Golf clubs,
balls
Level of Difficulty:
Moderate–advanced

This classic game (also known by its shorthand nickname, KP) has many entertaining variations. Play it any time, on almost any type of shot. If the players all lie off the green, see whose chip shot can get closest to the hole. Play it on sandtrap shots, long putts, or fairway shots where everyone has a fair chance of reaching the green. On a short par 3, play it on the first shot. But in order for the person to win, he or she must make par on the hole. Being closest to the pin should not be rewarded if it only earns the participant a bogey.

Closest to the Pin is a game within a game. Continue to record your strokes on the hole as usual; playing Closest to the Pin does not affect that. It is just an entertaining diversion during a round.

SCRAMBLE AND BEST BALL

Players: 4
Area: Golf course
Equipment: Golf clubs
Level of Difficulty:
Moderate–advanced

Scramble is a great group game. Everybody hits best ball. First everybody drives, then they all hit from where the best drive landed. Then they hit their approaches, followed by putts from wherever the best approach landed (assuming it made the green), and so forth until the ball goes into the hole. Scores can be very low in a scramble, and getting on in two and dropping it down in two more on a short par 4 is a very doable thing.

Best Ball is another entertaining game, though not on a par with Scramble. In the Best Ball format a person plays his or her own ball exclusively, and at the end of each hole the team score is the best individual score for that hole.

Skins

Players: 2–4
Area: Golf course
Equipment: Golf clubs
Level of Difficulty:
    Moderate–advanced

Gambling is as much a part of golf as bad lies and bogeys. Adults do it, so why not young people too? But, of course, they should keep the sums down to a reasonable level. Or—here's a thought—perhaps not use money at all! Bet tees, ball markers, or soft drinks.

Closest to the Pin, in all its manifestations, is a natural betting game. So too are many putting games. Longest Drive lends itself to a friendly wager or two, as does First on the Green. A high-rolling foursome could bet on Longest Drive, First on the Green, and Closest to the Hole on a single hole. It is not unheard-of for a player to win all the bets, but lose the hole.

Skins is one of the most famous of all betting games. The wager should be established prior to the beginning of the round. On the first hole, each member of the foursome pitches in a quarter. They then play the hole. The person who gets down in the fewest number of strokes wins a dollar and claims the skin. To win the money, a person must win the hole. A tie between two or more of the players carries the pot over to the next hole. Each person puts up a dime or a quarter at the start of each hole. If they halve the hole, the pot carries over and keeps building until someone wins a hole outright and claims all the money. When that happens, everybody chips in another quarter apiece and the pot starts building anew.

One-Club Golf

Players: 2–4
Area: Golf course
Equipment: Golf club of
    choice
Level of Difficulty:
    Advanced

Leave the bag at home, or at least in the trunk of the car, and play today with just one club. Any club will do: driver, putter, 9-iron, 3-wood. Just pick it and stay with it. Drive with the driver, chip with the driver, putt with the driver. It teaches resourcefulness and ingenuity. Or, if one club is too radical a departure, how about a 9-6-3 round? Play only with the 9-iron, 6-iron, 3-iron, and putter. Or try a different combination. This type of golf becomes grand fun with a half-dozen good friends on the course, each bashing away with their single club.

Obstacle Golf

Players: Unlimited
Area: Chipping green, open area
Equipment: Various obstacles, lots of balls, putter, sand wedge
Level of Difficulty: Advanced

Obstacle Golf requires some doing, but it is worth it. It is a team game, and golfers participate on relays.

The obstacles are restricted only by the imagination of the inventors. For example, the first station might be chipping. Players must chip through a horsecollar-shaped object up to, but not past, a row of milk carton crates on the green. Then, on the next station, they must chip over a ten-foot-high wooden barrier onto the green. Station No. 3 requires a flop shot over a bunker inside a garden hose encircling a hole on the green. Next is a bunker shot inside the hose. Then it is back to the crates, where the competitors must drop a putt from a spot marked by tees.

Each station consists of two identical obstacles, so that people compete side by side against each other. Lots and lots of balls—two piles at each station—are required to keep the relay moving without interruptions.

Obstacle Golf helps teach young players to make good decisions under pressure. In their rush to succeed, they almost always start out making harried, and inevitably faulty, shots. Only later do they learn the wisdom of the tortoise and slow down.

Ryder Wrong Cup

Players: Unlimited
Area: Golf course
Equipment: Golf clubs, balls
Level of Difficulty: Moderate–advanced

Golf is mostly an individual game, so give younger players a chance to play on a team and they will usually grab at it. The Ryder Cup is, of course, the biennial professional men's golf match between Europe and the United States. It is among the most successful events in golf because golfers play not for individual titles, but for the glory of their team. The Ryder Wrong Cup, a name coined by golf instructors Reamy Goodwin and Pat Pope, is one way to bring the same kind of team spirit to younger players.

If there are a group of players, divide them into two teams. Players from each team square off against one another in matches. These matches could last eighteen holes, or one hole. When one player wins, he wins a point for his team. At the end of the day, tally all the points and declare one side the winner.

It happens to players of all ages, of course, but it is particularly painful to see a youngster's game disintegrate over the course of a round. He may start strong, but then a bad shot will put a nick in his armor and before long he will become discouraged out of all proportion to what he has done. He will get down on himself and start making routinely poor shots. Worse, he will not care. But make this fellow play for something beyond his own individual score—for the greater good of his team—and it is a good bet that he will not let his game fall so completely apart. His backbone will turn to steel and he will reach inside himself for something that he has never found before, meanwhile gaining a deeper level of enjoyment and satisfaction from the day and perhaps even helping his team on to victory.

NINE

ICE HOCKEY

Fueled in part by the in-line skating boom, ice hockey is a growing sport in the United States. Youth hockey leagues are sprouting up in areas of the country that never see snow. While the games in this chapter are best suited for the ice, many of them will move easily onto the street or the playground for players using in-line skates.

For young skaters, hockey tag games are especially helpful. They teach coordination and improve a player's agility on skates. They help teach young players how to avoid other skaters and scramble up again after being knocked down. Games like Freeze Tag and Bumper Butts give youngsters a strong skating foundation for when they play with a stick and a puck. Just as young soccer players should touch the ball as much as possible, hockey players should handle the puck frequently. The more opportunities there are for a player to handle the puck, the quicker he will learn. Children should always wear gloves when playing ice hockey games.

Freeze Tag

Players: Unlimited
Area: Ice rink
Equipment: Skates,
  hockey gloves
Level of difficulty: Easy

Freeze Tag is as hilarious to watch as it is to play. It is a freewheeling tag game that helps youngsters with their agility on skates, their speed, and their ability to avoid skaters and other obstacles.

It might be wise to restrict Freeze Tag to a portion of the ice rather than using the entire rink. There can be one tagger or teams of taggers—whatever seems appropriate. The tagger skates after somebody and tags him, thereby "freezing" him in his spot. Then he goes off and tags somebody else. The game is over when everybody has been tagged.

However, there is one way to thaw out the frozen skaters. When a person is tagged, he stands on that spot with his legs wide apart. The only way he can get free is for another person—someone who is not frozen—to dive through his legs. Once somebody dives through his legs, that person is free to go off and unthaw other frozen people by diving through their legs as well.

Freeze Tag is a romp of a game. The kids are stopping, starting, falling down, getting up, sliding around—not unlike hockey itself.

Cops 'n' Robbers

Players: 2 teams of 10
  or more
Area: Ice rink
Equipment: Skates,
  hockey gloves
Level of Difficulty: Easy

Cops 'n' Robbers is another tag game that teaches youngsters agility, speed, and avoiding obstacles. The game is played over the entire ice. One team is the Cops, one team is the Robbers. The Robbers scatter first, followed shortly by the Cops in hot pursuit. The Cops chase the Robbers and after they tag them they bring them back behind their designated goal line to jail. That is where the Robbers must stay until one of their teammates flashes across the goal line, tags as many of his cohorts as he can, and they make a break for freedom.

Obviously, the Cops must try to stop this from occurring by patrolling in front of the jail area while others go in search of the fast-fleeing Robbers. The teams do not necessarily need to be composed of equal numbers on both sides; there could be twenty cops to fifteen robbers, or something of this sort.

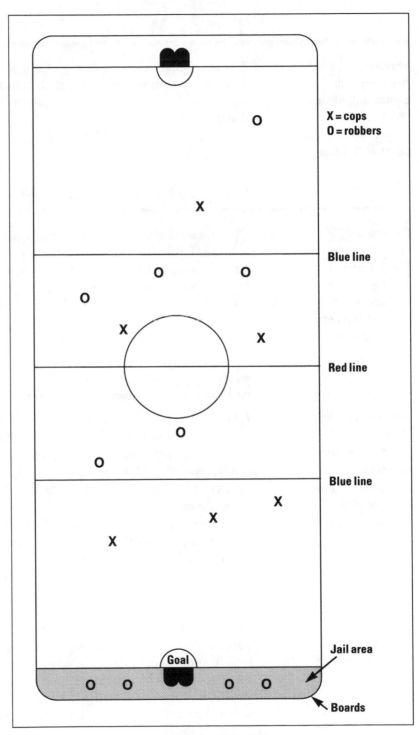

X = cops
O = robbers

Blue line

Red line

Blue line

Jail area

Goal

Boards

COPS 'N' ROBBERS

Tug of War

Players: 2
Area: Ice rink
Equipment: Skates,
hockey stick,
hockey gloves
Level of Difficulty: Easy

Instead of the traditional rope, play tug of war with a hockey stick. The two contestants see who can pull the other over onto the ice and take control of the stick, while developing their strength and balance on skates.

Stick Drill With a Purpose

Players: 2
Area: Ice rink
Equipment: Skates,
hockey gloves,
hockey stick
Level of Difficulty:
Moderate

Another balance game. One player swings a hockey stick back and forth on the ice while the other player tries to jump over it. The jumper jumps with both his feet which, as any young hockey player will affirm, is not so easy to do. At an appropriate time, the two switch roles.

Shuffle Races

Players: Unlimited
Area: Parking lot,
playground
Equipment: 5 traffic
cones, stopwatch
Level of Difficulty:
Easy–moderate

Shuffle Races help young players with their lateral movement and teach them to move their feet, something they will need to do in hockey and indeed in many other sports. The course is simple—five cones arranged in a fifteen-foot square. Place two of the cones at the top corners of the square, the three others at the bottom of the square, an equal distance apart.

Starting at the lower righthand corner of the square, a player runs up to the first cone, shuffles across (face forward) to the upper left cone, backpedals down to the bottom left of the square, shuffles across to the middle cone, and touches it. Then he retraces his steps: shuffling left, running up, shuffling right, then backpedaling to the start/finish cone.

By and large, young hockey players hate dryland training. They want to be on the ice, and dryland drills seem too much like work. But Shuffle Races and other such activities—standing long jump, hopping one-legged, jumping between tires—are vital to a youngster's development. They increase coordination and build strength, stamina, and speed. Obviously, the more fun these activities are—the more they resemble games rather than drills—the easier it will be to overcome juvenile resistance.

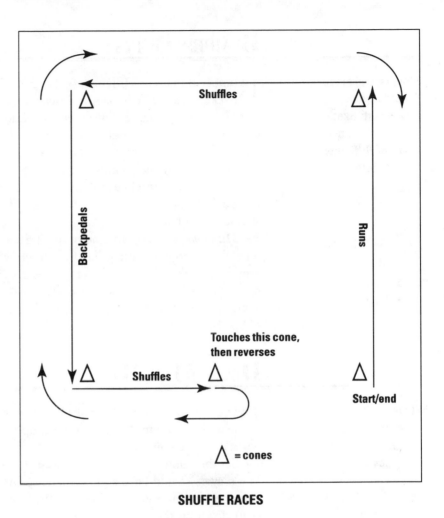

Backpedals

Shuffles

Runs

**Touches this cone,
then reverses**

Shuffles

Start/end

△ = cones

SHUFFLE RACES

Glove Relay

Players: Unlimited
Area: Parking lot, field
Equipment: Hockey
gloves for each
player, traffic cones
Level of Difficulty:
Easy–moderate

Glove Relay is a dryland game that builds conditioning. Divide the
players into teams of five or more and line them up behind the
starting line. Set the cones up about twenty yards away from the starting line, one cone per team. Each player on a team in turn runs up to
his team's cone, drops his glove, and returns to the starting line. The
glove pile grows with each runner. The last person in line runs up
to the cone, scoops up all his team's gloves, and carries them back to
his teammates. The first team to put on all their gloves and sit down,
wins.

BUMPER BUTTS

Players: Unlimited
Area: Ice rink
Equipment: Skates, hockey gloves
Level of Difficulty: Moderate

Bumper Butts is an aptly named tag game in which the players skate backward and knock people down with their rear ends. Everyone is It; there is no one tagger. The object is to knock the other person down. Once he is down, he is out for the game. Players must skate backward only and lead with their rear, as it were. The last person standing wins.

Bumper Butts helps kids learn how to hip-check, take a hit, skate backward, and skate while looking over their shoulder. The more people there are, the bigger the area for the game. With fewer players the space should be confined.

Other ways to play: Instead of skating backward, skate forward, and hit with the shoulder rather than the posterior. Players should keep their arms behind their backs and their gloves on. (Keeping the gloves on is a hard-and-fast rule for all hockey games.) Like Bumper Butts, this high-energy game will help youngsters grow accustomed to the sudden shocks of body-checking.

DIZZY MAN DRILL

Players: Unlimited
Area: Ice rink
Equipment: Skates, hockey gloves, traffic cones
Level of Difficulty: Moderate

Divide the players into two or more teams; four or five players on a team is optimum. Each team lines up single file, and all the teams begin from the same starting line.

Set the traffic cones about twenty-five yards from the starting line. The players should have a good, hard sprint to the cones, where they must perform a quite amusing (for the spectators) feat. Resting their head down on the cone, they must spin around the cone a specified number of times, then skate back to the start. Skate may be the wrong verb; "stagger" might be more apt, as the youngsters, dizzy and disoriented, find their way back to tag the next person in line, who must do the same whirlygig thing. It is a relay race, and the team that finishes first wins.

British Bulldog

Players: Unlimited
Area: Ice rink
Equipment: Skates, hockey gloves
Level of Difficulty: Moderate

British Bulldog is the ice hockey version of the camp game Pom Pom Tackoway. It will help kids learn how to skate faster, turn on a dime, stop suddenly, and avoid other skaters—all the while having a rollicking good time.

One person or three people or five people can be "It"—however many seems appropriate according to the size of the group. To begin the game the It person stands in the middle of the rink and shouts "Go!" thereby setting off a stampede to rival the Oklahoma Land Rush.

There could be five or fifty kids waiting at one end of the rink. At the signal, they take off en masse, trying to get to the other end without being tagged or tackled (whatever the coach prefers) by those in the middle. If a skater makes it to the end safely, he turns around and (at the coach's signal) skates back. If a skater is tagged, he becomes one of the It people—going to the center of the ice and helping to tag those still free.

Naturally, the number of taggers in the middle of the rink increases, while the number of people who are trying to avoid being tagged decreases. The skater who survives the longest without being tagged is the winner.

Street Hockey

Players: 2 or more
Area: Street, driveway
Equipment: Hockey sticks, tennis ball or homemade puck
Level of Difficulty: Moderate

Street Hockey has undergone a boom in recent years. Even adults are taking up the game. They may have played hockey in their youth and thanks to in-line skates, are now revisiting the game as a means of staying fit. For young people, the fact that adults are playing street hockey should not deter them from taking it up. Nor do they need a lot of high-priced, techno-fantastic gear to play. Street hockey is as simple and unpretentious a game as there is.

Essentially all that is required for a good game of Street Hockey is a pair of sneakers, a small rock, and a stick. The rock should be wrapped in tin foil so it slides on the paved surfaces. Some people may prefer to use a tennis ball, though balls do bounce around quite a bit.

The hockey stick can be made at home. Get an eight-foot sheet of ¾-inch or ⅝-inch plywood. Plywood works best because it is harder and won't break as easily. Softer woods such as pine break apart under the constant pounding of the street. Using a pencil, draw the stick (or sticks) on the sheet of plywood. Homemade sticks can be individually fitted to the size and age of the kids who will be wielding them. The longer the stick, the more susceptible it is to breaking. Cutting the stick out requires a saber saw or, if one is available, a jig saw. It might be advisable to employ Dad as construction consultant. Eventually the plywood laminate separates and breaks down; but the stick can be protected and its durability increased by wrapping duct tape or electrical tape around the striking end.

The rules of Street Hockey are very simple. Set up two goals at opposite ends of the designated playing area. (A couple of pieces of wood can serve as a goal, or draw the lines out with a piece of chalk.) It can be a one-on-one half-court game or a two-on-two game that takes place in the driveway. Or there can be lots of players and the game can range up and down the street. Each team tries to shoot the puck or ball past the goalie into the goal. Every goal scored counts for 1 point. There is no icing, no offsides, no referee. Body checking is allowed. Play fast, play fierce, play to win. Watch out for cars. Those are the rules of the street, and those are the rules of Street Hockey.

BROOM HOCKEY

Players: 2 teams of 5 or more
Area: Field, blacktop
Equipment: Brooms; rubber ball, volleyball, or Nerf ball
Level of Difficulty: Moderate

Like Street Hockey, Broom Hockey is an informal offspring of the ice game. College fraternities love it, though there is no reason why young children won't enjoy it as well. Play it like regular hockey, with two goals aligned at either end of a grassy field or blacktop surface. The rules should be flexible, for there is no reason to be formal—or particularly serious—about a game in which the hockey sticks are brooms and the puck is a small rubber ball. If some people don't have a broom to play with, use ordinary sticks and attach 2-liter plastic soda bottles to the ends. Then forget the rubber ball and use a volleyball. On pavement, try a small Nerf ball as a puck.

STICK RELAY

Players: Unlimited
Area: Ice rink
Equipment: Skates, hockey sticks, hockey gloves, traffic cones
Level of Difficulty: Moderate

Relay races are limited only by the imagination of those organizing and playing them. Stick Relay may have, let's say, ten players on a team. However many players there are, that's how many sticks each person must carry in the race. In this case the skater bundles ten sticks in his arms and takes off.

Where he goes and what he does next is, again, a matter for invention. With sticks in hand, the skater may be called upon to circle around a traffic cone, return to the starting line, and pass the sticks off to the next in line. Or he may do a spin, weave through a maze of cones, and perform a Superman-style dive onto the ice, all the while holding on to those precious hockey sticks.

Other ways to play: Obstacle races are another way to teach without teaching. A player starts in one corner of the rink and skates forward, then backward, in a circle. From there it is up along the boards, zigzagging through traffic cones. At the other end of the ice, two cones support a hockey stick placed between them. The skater does a Superman dive under the stick, gets up, spins in backward and forward circles, and sprints back to the place where he started. How quickly a person can get to his skates after a fall can make a big difference in hockey. Obstacle races help foster that ability.

HOCKEY RACES

Players: Teams of 2
Area: Ice rink
Equipment: Skates, hockey gloves, hockey sticks
Level of Difficulty: Moderate

Hockey really lends itself to fun, educational relay races in which the players can work on skills while they're having a good time. For example, one player skates with one leg in the air up to the red line. As he does so, he carries both his stick and his partner's stick in his arms. When he returns to the goal line where he began, he hands off the sticks to his partner, who, thus encumbered, takes off one-legged on his own.

Another idea: This is a variation on the old-fashioned wheelbarrow race. One skater pulls another skater on his knees using their sticks (blades forward). They go up to the red line, return, trade places, and do it again. A hilarious variation calls for one person to lie flat on his stomach and hang onto the sticks while his partner drags him down the ice. The puller must really dig into the ice to get the dead weight behind him moving. Sometimes, of course, smaller players cannot pull their bigger partners and a coach must step in to help.

It is even funnier to watch a threesome try this race. One player pulls, a second lies flat while hanging onto the sticks, and a third, also being dragged down the ice on his belly, hangs onto the second player by his ankles.

Floor Hockey

Players: 2 teams of 6 or more

Area: Gym, playground, or athletic field

Equipment: Hockey sticks, optional safety equipment, ball or puck, 2 goal nets or 4 traffic cones

Level of Difficulty: Moderate–advanced

Floor hockey is basically hockey in sneakers. Ideally, there are six people on a side, but as many as ten people can play on a team. With fewer players there tends to be less bunching in the center of the court, adding to the game's speed and high-energy movement.

One of the appeals of floor hockey is that it can be played indoors or out. A basketball court can be the playing area in a gymnasium, with the goals at either end. Outside, on the blacktop at school, the basketball courts can serve as guide; the width of four courts side by side is about the length of a hockey field. In any case, make the playing area about twice as long as it is wide. Be resourceful. If there are no nets handy to use as goals, set up two pairs of traffic cones—or anything else that is suitable—about six to twelve feet apart. Mark the playing field boundaries clearly with chalk so that everybody can see them.

The rules of floor hockey are the same as in the NHL except: (1) There are no offsides calls, (2) Body checking is not allowed, and (3) The game will not be stopped for ten minutes while two of the competitors engage in a fistfight. Face-offs after a score should be kept under control. Players can use their feet to kick the puck, but they can't kick a puck into a goal to score. Just as in the ice game, only the goalie can use his hands. Assess penalties for high-sticking; bringing the stick above the waist is forbidden. A high-sticking penalty means the loss of the puck or a time-out on the bench if it's a serious violation.

Floor hockey is a snap to learn. Just take that stick and whack that puck. One team starts things off from the center line and the game naturally proceeds from there. A puck is not always a puck in floor hockey; sometimes it's a ball. Sometimes on the blacktop a puck can get turned on its edge and with a good gust of wind take off on its own, independent of the actions of the players. A rubber ball is a better bet, though it can roll quite a bit too. A weighted ball that allows the players to flash along the sidelines like Mario Lemieux, sliding the ball as if it were really a puck on ice, is the best of all.

Safety equipment for serious floor hockey games is a good idea. Those with glasses should wear protective shields; eye protection and mouthguards are a good idea. Helmets, gloves, and other protective equipment for the goalies are also prudent.

ZONE HOCKEY

Players: 2 teams of 10–12 players

Area: Playground or gym

Equipment: Hockey sticks, optional safety equipment, ball or puck, 2 goal nets or 4 traffic cones

Level of Difficulty: Moderate–advanced

Zone Hockey is similar to Floor Hockey. The principle variation is that instead of running around all over the court as they do in Floor Hockey, players stick to designated zones.

Zone Hockey is a good game for when there are lots of people who want to play. It gives the players a feel for what it's like to play the different positions on a hockey team. With twelve players on a team, four play forward, four play center, and four defense. The position of goalie is usually left out of Zone Hockey, because there are plenty of defenders hanging around the goal already.

Players pass, handle their sticks, and advance the puck just as they do in Floor Hockey, except they must always stay within their respective areas. The forwards stay near the opposing team's goal, the centers occupy the middle area of the court and put the puck in play after a goal, and the defenders protect their net from sallies by their opponents. It's best to rotate positions on a team so that at the end of each game every player has had a chance to test his skills as a defender, a forward, and a center at least once.

ONE-ON-ONE
(TWO-ON-TWO, FOUR-ON-FOUR)

Players: Unlimited

Area: Ice rink

Equipment: Skates, hockey gloves, hockey sticks, pucks

Level of Difficulty: Advanced

This set of games is an excellent example of the building-block approach to teaching sports to young people. One-on-One leads to Two-on-Two, which flows easily into Four-on-Four.

Two groups of players line up on one side of the rink. The coach shoots the puck along the red line across the ice against the boards. The two players—one from each group—race for the puck. The one who gains control goes on offense, taking the puck to the net opposite from the line he was in. His opponent plays defense and tries to stop him from getting a clear shot on goal. After one shot on goal, the players return to the end of their respective lines. Goalies defend each net.

The coach should frequently send pucks—hence, skaters—zipping across the ice. The lines keep moving and the ice fills with dueling mini-Gretzkys. The ice gets even busier when the one-on-one games become two-on-two—two skaters from each line fighting over the puck, working their sticks, advancing on the goalie, and firing.

The four-on-four game is a mini-scrimmage on full ice. The two

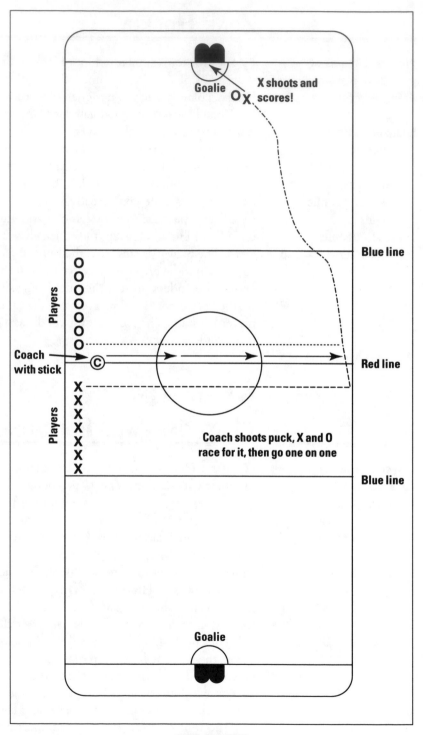

ONE-ON-ONE

teams should play for a goodly duration. When the coach blows his whistle, the skaters leave the puck where it lies and the next two teams race for it to start their game.

Two-on-One

Players: 3
Area: Ice rink
Equipment: Skates,
hockey gloves,
hockey sticks, puck
Level of Difficulty:
Advanced

This game is played around the net. The "two" are skaters and the "one" is a goalie. The skaters work together to create shots and the goalie works to stop them. The skaters charge into the goal, pass, pull out, slice forward, glide behind the net. The goalie moves with them, always watchful, ready to respond when the others make their attack. Two-on-One can be played even during a team scrimmage, in that lull period for the goalie when the teams are at the opposite net.

Scrimmage Games

Players: Unlimited
Area: Ice rink
Equipment: Skates,
hockey gloves,
hockey sticks,
pucks
Level of Difficulty:
Advanced

Like obstacle and relay races, scrimmage games can provide exercise for the imagination in addition to practicing basic hockey skills. A coach could easily set up a one-on-one match at one end of the ice and a three-on-three at the other, while a two-on-two game takes place at center ice.

But don't just have them play regular hockey; fool around a little! For the one-on-one game, the players should skate backwards. Backward skating will help them with their stick-handling and backhand shot, not to mention their backward maneuvering. For the foursome at center ice, tell them to turn their sticks around so they're controlling the puck with the knob. And as for that three-on-three game, don't let the players skate more than four feet without making a pass. If they don't pass, they forfeit the puck. This will help teach them to keep their head up and look for the open man.

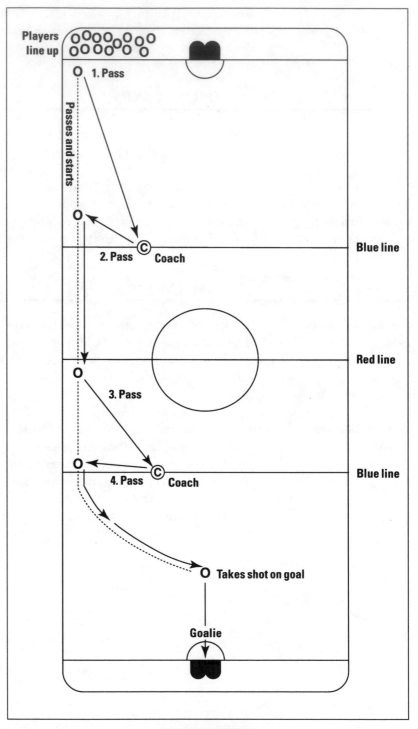

PASS AND SHOOT

PASS AND SHOOT

Players: Unlimited
Area: Ice rink
Equipment: Skates,
hockey gloves,
hockey sticks,
pucks
Level of Difficulty:
Advanced

Pass and Shoot combines essential hockey skills in a more challenging way. The players line up at one end of the ice. Each, in turn, begins with a puck and passes it to a coach stationed at the blue line. The coach passes it back to the player as he skates up the ice along the boards. He then passes to the next coach stationed at the second blue line. This coach sharply returns it and the player moves in for a shot on goal. After his shot the player goes into the line forming at the end of the ice opposite from where he started. When all the players have gone through, they turn around and play Pass and Shoot the other way. Coaches get a workout in this game along with their players.

TEN

LACROSSE

Lacrosse is a sport with ancient roots; historians believe that American Indians were the first to play it. It survives to this day as a club and school sport similar in many respects to field hockey.

Lacrosse is a wide-open field game—indeed, Indian braves played it without boundaries—in which ceaselessly moving teams of players transport a ball by carrying it, passing it, or kicking it. The object of all this activity is, of course, to score goals. The play is complicated by the fact that all of the catching and throwing in lacrosse must be done with a lacrosse stick. Because catching and throwing are so central to the sport, the games in this chapter focus on the development of these skills.

STOPS AND STARTS

Players: Unlimited
Area: Playing field or open area
Equipment: Lacrosse sticks and balls
Level of Difficulty: Easy

Stops and Starts is a simple way to get youngsters accustomed to carrying a ball with those unusual-looking lacrosse sticks. Players begin on a line together. On the coach's whistle, they run forward carrying the balls with their sticks. The whistle blows again and they run backward. Then sideways to the left, then sideways to the right. Playing lacrosse demands quick footwork and rapid changes of directions. Stops and

Starts is an exuberant group activity that introduces these skills to players who are new to the game.

HOT POTATO

Players: Unlimited
Area: Playing field or open area
Equipment: Lacrosse sticks and balls
Level of Difficulty: Easy–moderate

So many traditional children's games—Duck Duck Goose, Steal the Bacon, Paper Rock Scissors—can be easily adapted to sports. Hot Potato works particularly well with lacrosse, helping to improve passing skills and teamwork. Instead of a potato, use a lacrosse ball. The players form a circle and pass the ball around with their sticks. At the end of a pre-established time (fifteen or thirty seconds or whatever), the coach yells "Stop!" and whoever gets caught with the ball must leave the game. (For a special twist, coaches may even want to bring a boom box and let the players pass the ball to musical accompaniment. When the music stops, just as in the children's game of Hot Potato, the player with the ball is out.) If a player flubs a catch and is chasing the ball when the music stops, he is out, too. One by one the players are eliminated until the winner is crowned.

SUCCESS

Players: Unlimited
Area: Playing field or open area
Equipment: Lacrosse sticks and balls
Level of Difficulty: Easy–moderate

Success is a lacrosse version of the sandlot baseball game Three Flies—Up! (page 39). One player starts as thrower. With his lacrosse stick he throws either a high fly ball or a grounder to a group of players in the field. If a player catches the ball in the air or snags it cleanly on the ground, he becomes the thrower. In lacrosse, unlike Three Flies—Up!, just one successful catch earns a person the right to exchange positions.

However, if nobody catches or fields the ball, there is still a way to become the thrower. The person in the field who picks up the ball tosses it in to the thrower, who lays his stick on the ground at his feet. If the ball hits the stick, the person who threw it gets to become the thrower. If the ball misses, the thrower gets another turn.

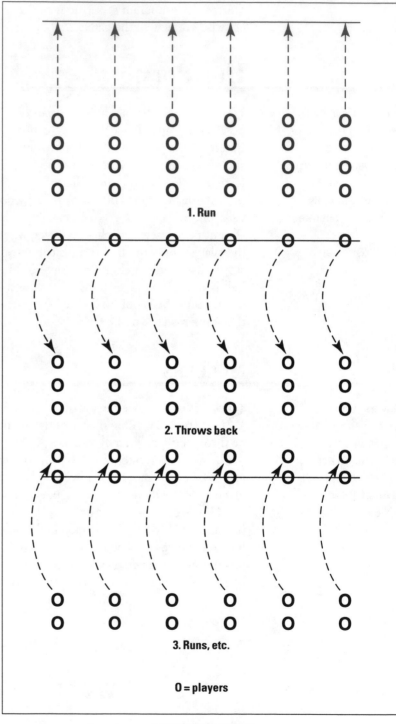

1. Run

2. Throws back

3. Runs, etc.

O = players

LONG PASS RELAY

Wall Ball (Lacrosse)

Players: Unlimited
Area: Playing field or open area
Equipment: Lacrosse sticks and balls
Level of difficulty: Moderate

Wall Ball is a playground game (described on page 190) in which two players compete against each other by bouncing or kicking a ball against a wall. The game is especially suitable for lacrosse because it helps teach players how to throw and catch.

The players stand behind a line about ten to fifteen feet from a wall; they cannot throw the ball too low, or it will be impossible to catch. The number of times the ball can bounce after it strikes the wall depends on the ages and skills of the players. Advanced players should field it in the air; others might need a bounce or two before they can catch it. If the ball bounces (or bounces more than the allowed number of times), the player who tossed it scores a point. Game goes to 12.

If there is a large group of players, it may be better to shuttle the players in and out depending on who wins the point. Two players square off. The loser goes to the end of the line, while the winner stays on to play the next in line. If the challenger wins, he stays and the former champion goes to the end of the line, etc.

Long Pass Relay

Players: Unlimited
Area: Playing field or open area
Equipment: Lacrosse sticks and balls
Level of Difficulty: Moderate–advanced

For this excellent conditioning relay that practices cradling the ball, pivoting, passing, and catching, divide the players into teams and line them up single file. At the whistle, the first members of each team race up to a line twenty yards away. When they reach this line they turn and throw back to the next person in line, who must catch it and herself run to the designated line. Then she turns and throws back to the next person, etc. If a player loses the ball while she is running, she simply picks it up and keeps going. The same if she misses the catch. The first team to gather all of its players at the designated line wins.

ELEVEN

SOCCER

Soccer is unique in that children can begin playing it at a very early age and enjoy success. Four- and five-year-olds who cannot tie their shoes can still play a munchkin version of the game. They not only have fun, but they walk away with pride in their achievements on the field. This may be why soccer is so popular with young people.

Soccer games may be the most creative of any sport in the U.S. This may simply be out of necessity, because even though it is the world's most popular sport, soccer is still largely unfamiliar to many citizens of this country. One common thread in all the soccer games in this chapter is the recognition that every player should touch the ball as much as possible. A youngster's development in soccer proceeds in tandem with the closeness of her relationship to the ball. The more touches, the more learning takes place. Gradually the player develops a kinship with the ball and before long she is doing the most astonishing things with it.

INDOOR SOCCER

Indoor Soccer is played in the winter months in gymnasiums, rec centers, YMCAs, school auditoriums, and church and community centers. Older children can play Indoor Soccer, but it is especially good for the very young.

The rules for Indoor Soccer are basically the same as for the outdoor game, although the size and potential idiosyncracies of the playing area underline the need for flexible rules. So, too, do the ages of the players. Keeping score is an option that many coaches may wish to forego. Winning and losing are not fundamental to an appreciation of Indoor Soccer.

One of the greatest appeals of soccer is that boys and girls can play together on an equal footing. The number of boys and girls on a side depends on the size of the playing area. Shin guards or long pants are a must, for an indoor soccer ball draws children to it like a magnet. When the players cluster around the ball, their little feet get going and they frequently do not connect with their intended target.

There may not be room for a net. If that's the case, two orange traffic cones about fifteen feet apart—the width of the base of a basketball key—will work just fine. No score will be allowed if the ball crosses high above the goal; the ball must roll through the cones on the ground or pass through no higher than the height of the pint-sized goalie.

Free substitution should be the order of the day, and the not-so-good players should play as much as the good ones. If a really good player is dominating events, after a while she should move into the goal to limit her influence.

BUNNIES AND HUNTERS

Bunnies and Hunters is an elementary version of Cat and Mouse-type soccer games that will be described later in the chapter. The hunters are the shooters; they stand along the sides of a rectangular area of play. They have balls, and they practice their kicking by trying to hit the bunnies as the bunnies pass between them. They can shoot as often as they like. When a bunny gets hit, he or she just keeps hopping to the end, or goes out. The size of the area depends on the ages and skills of the players, though this game is intended for the littlest ones. The bunnies have a good time because they actually get to hop-hop-hop while the hunters fire away (and mostly miss).

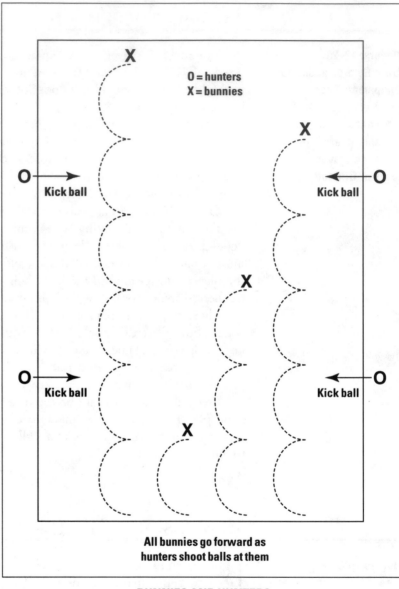

O = hunters
X = bunnies

Kick ball

Kick ball

Kick ball

Kick ball

All bunnies go forward as
hunters shoot balls at them

BUNNIES AND HUNTERS

BULLDOG

Players: 5–8
Area: Portion of soccer field
Equipment: Soccer balls
Level of Difficulty: Easy

Like Bunnies and Hunters, Bulldog is an elementary version of more advanced soccer games. Five or six players stand in a row, each with a ball. One player without a ball—the bulldog—stands ten feet away from them in the middle of a defined area. The players with balls try to dribble past the bulldog to a designated safe area. The bulldog tries to disrupt the dribblers and steal their balls. A player whose ball gets stolen or knocked away can either become a bulldog herself or watch from the sidelines as others get picked off. In the latter case, after all the players lose their balls, a new bulldog is chosen and the game starts over.

HEAD CATCH

Players: 4–8 (including a coach)
Area: Open area
Equipment: Soccer ball
Level of Difficulty: Easy

Circle games in soccer are endlessly varied. Just form a circle, add a ball or two, and nearly everybody can come up with a game that is creative and entertaining.

Head Catch is a circle game that teaches fast thinking. Four to eight players stand in a circle with a coach in the center. The coach makes short, soft tosses to each, moving around the circle. The coach can make repeated tosses to a player, if the coach is so inclined. As the coach makes the toss he calls out "Head" or "Catch," and the player must do the *opposite* of the command. If the coach calls "Catch," the player must head the ball back to him; if the coach calls "Head," the player must catch it. If the player doesn't do the right thing he or she sits down. Head Catch should move quickly, with the ball popping back and forth between coach and players. The winner is the last one standing.

SOCCER DUCK DUCK GOOSE

Players: 5–10
Area: Open area
Equipment: 1 soccer ball for each player
Level of Difficulty: Easy

Duck Duck Goose is a traditional children's game. One child walks around the circle saying "Duck, duck" as she taps the children seated on the ground on the head. Then she picks someone by tapping him and saying "Goose," and the two race around the circle to be first to the spot vacated by the person who was picked. By adding a ball to this game, Soccer Duck Duck Goose becomes an excellent way to teach youngsters how to dribble.

In the best soccer games, everyone has a ball or is touching one constantly. The player who begins the game dribbles a ball around the circle. She may or may not want to chant the "Duck, duck" mantra; that is up to the group. After she tags one of the players on the ground, they race around the circle, each dribbling a ball. The tagger tries to make it around the circle and fill the empty spot, vacated by the person who was tagged. If she makes it to the spot first, the new person becomes the tagger. If she fails to make it, she remains the tagger and tries again.

It may be that the players are very young and can't dribble very well. If this is the case, put a ball in the center of the circle. The children play the game in the traditional way, but they race around the circle to retrieve the ball in the center. The person who gets there first tries to dribble it back to the empty spot in the circle, while the other person defends against it.

If a soccer coach attempts to play this with a group of twelve-year-olds, he may be inviting open rebellion. Nevertheless, it is good fun—and good dribbling practice—for the little ones.

Soccer Stop and Go!

Players: Unlimited
Area: Portion of soccer field
Equipment: 1 soccer ball for each player
Level of Difficulty: Easy

Red Light Green Light is one of the oldest and simplest of children's games. And it converts easily into a game for either soccer or basketball. We have updated the name to Stop and Go!, but the rules are the same. A coach (or perhaps a player) stands with his back turned to the players who are going to try to make their way up to him. They might be twenty-five or thirty yards away on a soccer field. The person with his back turned yells "Go!," and the players dribble a ball toward him. When he yells "Stop!" all the players must stop. If, as he turns, he spots someone moving, that person must return to the starting line. The caller turns his back again, issues the "Go" command, and the players move forward once more. The player who dribbles the ball all the way up to the caller first wins.

Saddle Up!

Players: Unlimited
Area: Portion of soccer field
Equipment: Soccer balls
Level of Difficulty: All levels

Saddle Up! is a terrific game because all ages and abilities can have fun playing it. Everyone pairs off and forms a circle. The size of the circle depends on how many players there are and how far the instructor wants them to run. All the balls are placed in the middle of the circle—one ball per pair to start.

One member of each pair competes at a time. When the instructor says "Saddle Up!" the designated person jumps onto the back of his

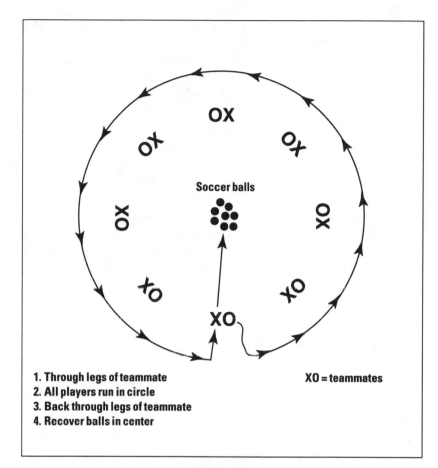

Soccer balls

1. **Through legs of teammate**
2. **All players run in circle**
3. **Back through legs of teammate**
4. **Recover balls in center**

XO = teammates

SADDLE UP!

partner in the manner of a piggyback ride. If either partner is too big for the other, then he should simply rest his hands on the back of his partner's shoulders, with the partner facing the center of the circle. After everyone is saddled up, the instructor yells "Go!" and the race begins. The competing member of each pair drops to the ground, scrambles through his partner's legs, and begins running around the outside of the circle.

Everybody runs in the same direction and as fast as they can. Saddle Up! is excellent for a mixed group because five-year-olds can play along-side twelve-year-olds. Though the little ones cannot keep up, they still have a great time running with the bigger kids. After the runners make a full circle and return to their partners, they again scramble through their partner's legs and run into the center of the circle where the balls are. There, they gather up a ball and dribble it back to their partner to finish their portion of the race. When this group is finished running, the instructor gives the "Saddle Up!" command again and the partners get their turn to do the same thing.

After each group has had at least one round, the instructor removes one ball from the circle to make the game competitive. The coach should rely on his or her judgment on when to remove a ball. Everybody should feel the satisfaction at least once of running the circle and at the end of their big effort, finding a ball to dribble.

With one ball missing, a runner will come up empty at the end of his or her run. This eliminates her team and they sit down. Take away a second ball for the next round and at the end of the run, another team will sit down. And so forth until two finalists compete to be Saddle Up! champion. Even after the competition begins, the five-year-olds can play. They are of course eliminated in an early round, but they love running around so much and jumping on their partner's back (usually a coach) that they will hardly notice that their ball is missing. Eventually, they get tired and sit down to watch the competition with the rest of the players.

Cow Patties

Players: Unlimited
Area: Portion of soccer field
Equipment: Lots and lots of soccer balls, traffic cones
Level of Difficulty: Easy

Cow Patties is a tag game. Children improve their agility and quickness as they try to avoid not only soccer balls on the ground but other players as well.

Cow Patties should be played in an area sized proportionately to the number of players, marked off with traffic cones. The ten to fifty kids who can play must run from end to end without touching one of the dozens of balls, or "cow patties," scattered across the ground. Balls should be everywhere, as many as are available. The more balls there are, the more difficult it will be for the players, or "cowboys," to dodge, step, jump, and move around them. The coach starts the group running with a whistle or a shout.

Inevitably, one or more of the players will graze a ball on their run-through. After someone touches a ball he becomes a cow patty and must, from a kneeling position, stretch and reach and lunge for the others coming through on the next run. When he makes a touch, that person joins him on his knees as a cow patty, and their numbers gradually multiply. While avoiding the living cow patties, the cowboys must still be sure to miss the inanimate ones—the soccer balls.

It may be that a couple of players need to be assigned to be cow patties right at the start to help get the game going. If a cowboy runs outside the boundary lines, he becomes a cow patty. And if he lingers too long at the start, hoping to pick his way more cautiously through a landscape littered with soccer balls and lunging children, that can turn him into a cow patty too.

CRAB SOCCER

Players: 5 or more
Area: Portion of soccer field
Equipment: 1 soccer ball for each player
Level of Difficulty: Easy–moderate

Crab Soccer builds upper body strength, improves dribbling, and creates teamwork. As usual, the size of the playing area depends on the number of players. The game can take place inside a small circle or a grid within the larger field. Everybody starts with a ball except for the designated "crab," who chases after the other players on his feet and hands with his chest and knees pointing skyward.

The crab's job is to kick the ball away from the others. Considering the awkwardness of his stance, the crab accomplishes this with quite astonishing bursts of speed and agility. When a crab kicks a dribbler's ball away, that person becomes a crab too. Now there are two crabs skittering about, kicking at balls. Finally only the best dribbler is left, and all the crabs gang up on him.

Other ways to play: Another form of Crab Soccer makes not just one player the crab, but all the players. Two teams of players, all in the crab position, play a soccer game within the designated area. Crab-dribbling is not easy, but it is amazing what young bodies can do!

OBSTACLE GAMES

Players: Unlimited
Area: Portion of soccer field
Equipment: 1 soccer ball for each player, obstacles (be inventive!)
Level of Difficulty: Easy–moderate

Obstacle Games are a fun warm-up and a good way to get the juices flowing before practice. There is no one way to set up an obstacle course; it depends, of course, on the type of obstacles available and the playing area. The most practical advice is this: Don't be practical.

Hula hoops make excellent obstacles. Lay one on the ground and let the players kick into it—or set it up upright and let them kick through it. For one test, have a player swing the hoop around his body while performing a header. Traffic cones, of course, work well too. Players can dribble through the cones in zigzag patterns or any other challenging pattern. Are there garbage cans around the field? Have the players kick over one or even into it. Players may also dribble up and down the stadium steps, kick through the football goalposts, or hop over a bench on its side. Players may compete individually or as members of a team, or the entire group can be on the same side and compile a cumulative score.

Cat and Mouse

Players: Unlimited
Area: Portion of soccer field
Equipment: Soccer balls, traffic cones (optional)
Level of Difficulty: Easy–moderate

One test of a good game may be the number of variations it spawns. Cat and Mouse passes this test with flying colors, for there seems to be an endless variety of games based on its basic chase-and-catch theme.

One Cat and Mouse game features a line of players (the mice) running between two points while another group of players (the cats) tries to hit them with a kicked ball. (This is similar to Bunnies and Hunters.) If the mice make it into their "hole" without being touched, they get to run again. The mice should run in a straight line across the cats' field of vision, with the distances set up so that runners and kickers have an equal chance at success.

Another form of Cat and Mouse is similar to the famous swimming game, Sharks and Minnows. One player stands at one end of a designated area, the other players stand opposite him a reasonable distance away. When the whistle blows the mice run en masse toward a line just past where the cat is standing. If they make it beyond the line to the safe zone, they remain mice. If the cat touches them with a kicked ball, they get a ball of their own and become a cat themselves, trying to capture a mouse on the next pass.

One more variation: Set up an area with traffic cones at the four corners. Four players with balls—these are the cats—chase the rest of the players within the designated area. The cats catch the mice by touching them below the waist with their balls. When a mouse gets caught, he or she stands by the cone that the cat claimed as his own at the start of the game. The cat who captures the most mice wins.

Triangle Games

Players: 3 or 4
Area: Portion of soccer field
Equipment: Soccer ball, traffic cones
Level of Difficulty: Moderate

Triangle Games lay a foundation for much of what happens on a soccer field. They make players think a step ahead: Am I going to get the ball? What do I do with it once I get it?

The games take place on a rectangular grid with three players positioned at three corners on the grid. These three form the human triangle that shifts constantly with their movements. Two players at the corners of the grid flank the player with the ball at all times. The corners of the grid can be marked with traffic cones.

The game consists of passing and moving, passing and moving. Players learn to anticipate what the person with the ball will do, and move correspondingly. To start, one player kicks to another. The third player

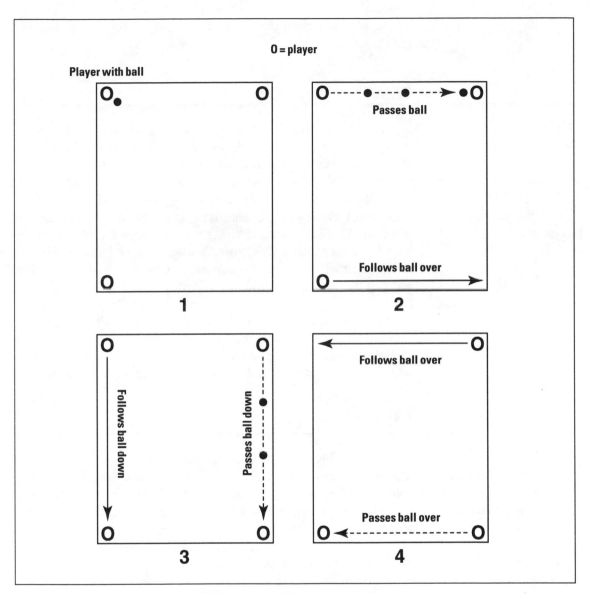

SEQUENCE OF 4 TRIANGLE MOVEMENTS

moves with the ball along the grid, thus shifting the triangle. The second player kicks to the third and the first player moves, forming a new triangle. Now the third player quickly kicks to the first, and so on.

Add a fourth player to the mix and create a fascinating game of keepaway. The threesome on the grid do the same as before, passing and shifting with the ball, but now there is a person in the middle trying to steal it. If he succeeds in intercepting or deflecting a pass, he moves to a corner and the player whose pass he intercepted becomes the chaser.

SPACE INVADERS

Players: 10–15
Area: Portion of soccer field
Equipment: 1 soccer ball for each player, traffic cones
Level of Difficulty: Moderate

Establish a rectangular grid, with players lined up on each side. Set seven or so traffic cones—the number is purely arbitrary—down the center of this twenty-yard-long area. Everybody has a ball to start.

At one end of the grid is the "space monster." The monster is actually a player who tries to dribble through all the cones while avoiding the balls being kicked by the players on the sides. These players, it should be noted, are Defenders of Earth trying to shoot down the monster before it lands on this planet and destroys Civilization as we know it. (Hey, if it works, use it.) The defenders can hit either the monster or its ball. Whoever hits the monster takes its place and tries to become ravager of Planet Earth.

Space Invaders is great for foot-eye coordination. Players learn how to lead their passes, and anticipate where a ball is coming from and going to. If dribbling is too difficult for some, eliminate the dribble and let the monster simply run through the cones while dodging the incoming balls.

OUTER SPACE

Players: 8–16
Area: Portion of soccer field
Equipment: 2 traffic cones and 1 soccer ball for every 2 players
Level of Difficulty: Moderate

Like Space Invaders, Outer Space takes place on a grid. Line up an equal number of players across from one another with each player paired with the person opposite him. In the center between the two lines, set up two cones for each team. There should be a reasonable amount of space between the cones, for the players try to kick the ball through them to their partners. If they hit the cones or miss entirely, a coach or coaches can kick the ball to "outer space"—that is, wherever he likes. Young people derive inordinate glee from seeing the other team's balls kicked into orbit, and they even enjoy giving chase to their own balls when it happens to them.

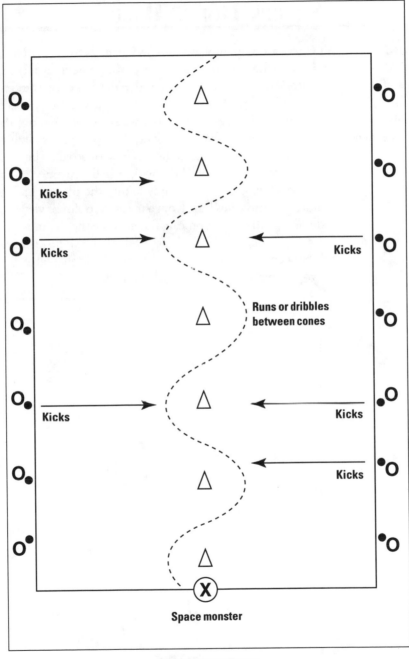

SPACE INVADERS

SOCCER DODGE BALL

Players: Unlimited
Area: Soccer field
Equipment: Lots of
soccer balls
Level of Difficulty:
Moderate–advanced

There are as many variations and formats to Soccer Dodge Ball as there are to the playground version of the game. Play it the traditional way, with one team of players clustered in the center of a circle, the other team on the outside shooting the balls at them. This being soccer, the shooters must hit their targets below the waist by kicking, not throwing. When the kickers knock everybody out, the two teams switch roles.

Or let everybody into the circle with a ball. The object is to knock players out by kicking them with a ball. Anyone touched by another person's ball is out. But simply letting the players kick balls at one another accomplishes little from a teaching point of view; so establish conditions. Before a person can aim at someone, he must touch the ball to his thigh, followed by his head. Only then can he kick at another player. If he succeeds in putting the player out, he must once again perform the two touches before renewing his attack.

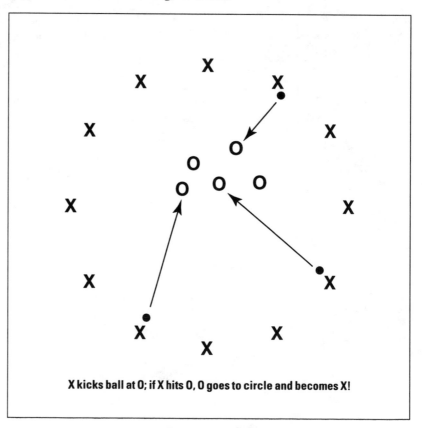

X kicks ball at O; if X hits O, O goes to circle and becomes X!

SOCCER DODGE BALL

CHIPPING GAME

Players: 2 teams of 4
Area: Soccer field
Equipment: Soccer balls
for players, goal
with no net
Level of Difficulty:
Moderate–advanced

Line up the two teams on opposite sides of a goal with no net. How far the players stand from the goal depends on their age and abilities. If the penalty line is too far out for them, they can shoot from the goal box line—eight yards out—just to get the game going.

The players aim for the crossbar with their shots; when they hit it their team scores. Only hitting the crossbar makes a score; hitting the sideposts does not count. Balls go wide, balls go high. Since there is no net (and no goalie), balls are flying back and forth. Players cannot retrieve any balls with their hands; if they do their team is penalized a point. Teams play to 5 or 10, and learn trapping and shooting skills as they do.

WEMBLEY WAY

Players: 10–20
Area: Portion of soccer
field
Equipment: Soccer balls,
goal, traffic cones
(optional)
Level of Difficulty:
Moderate–advanced

Wembley Way offers an enchanting array of possibilities for the young soccer player. It is played on a rectangular grid, with traffic cones at the corners. In the center of the base of the grid is the goal, where the coach stands. The players form two equal-sized teams and line up on each side of the goal at the bottom of the grid. Each player on a team is assigned a number, with the two teams having corresponding numbers, and the action proceeds from there. (A more difficult version of the game places several cones in a line along each side of the grid.)

When the coach calls out a number, the players from each team who have that number compete in a dribbling race up the side lines. (For a more difficult game, the players must dribble between cones.) When they finish the course they dribble along the top of the grid and turn down though two soccer balls that can serve as the gateway to the playing field. The dueling contestants then fire on the goal and whoever makes it, scores a point for his or her team.

When assigning numbers, coaches should try to match up players of equal abilities so when a number is called, the two players will give each other a good go.

This version of Wembley Way practices dribbling and turns. Youngsters learn to look up, not be absorbed with the ball and their feet—a bad habit—because they desperately want to keep tabs on the person they're racing. Things get more interesting when the coach calls out two (or three or five) numbers at a time, making all those players respond at once. When all the numbers get called at the same time, a madcap scramble ensues.

Other ways to play: For younger players, it may be wise to eliminate the dribbling element and let them just run. After they run up the side and through the two balls, the coach should roll a ball on the ground in front of the net. The two contestants go for the ball, and the one who gets to it first and shoots it into the net, scores a point for his team.

Or maybe ask the players to go through "the gate"—the two balls—in unusual ways, such as crawling through it on their bellies, or crab-style. Or assign two players to hold a pole or a stick at the gate, requiring each contestant to do the limbo before passing through.

KING OF THE DRIBBLERS

Players: Unlimited
Area: Portion of soccer field or open area
Equipment: 1 soccer ball for each player
Level of Difficulty: Moderate–advanced

A classic soccer game, King of the Dribblers teaches youngsters how to move with the ball. Play it with five to twenty-five children in a designated area. All the players must stay within the boundaries.

Each player dribbles a ball. While dribbling, he or she tries to kick away everybody else's ball. A person goes out if he loses his ball or it gets kicked outside the area of play. When only two players remain, they square off to determine the King of the Dribblers.

SHARK

Players: Unlimited
Area: Portion of soccer field or open area
Equipment: 1 soccer ball for each player
Level of Difficulty: Advanced

Shark is a more advanced version of King of the Dribblers. In one version of Shark also known as Jaws, all but one of the players dribble balls within a defined area which they cannot leave. One player on the outside—the shark—does not have a ball. Suddenly he rushes into the area and causes pandemonium, kicking away balls while the dribblers try to stay away from him, practicing their turning as they do. When a person's ball gets kicked out, the ball stays out but the person stays in and joins the shark pack. Soon all the players are fighting for control over the one remaining ball, and this can get *very* intense.

For more advanced players, let the shark dribble a ball as well. He still tries to knock balls away, but he must do this while controlling one of his own. The shark must have good ball-control skills and be able to pass accurately.

In another variation called Tigers in a Jungle, the shark—now transformed into a tiger—attacks on his hands and knees. When he knocks away the balls of the dribblers, they become tigers and go onto their hands and knees too.

DETECTIVE

Players: 6–10
Area: Portion of soccer field or open area
Equipment: 1 soccer ball for each player
Level of Difficulty: Advanced

Detective is another variation on the Shark theme, but with enough of a twist to merit its own write-up. Play it like Shark except in this game the shark is a detective and the dribblers are all robbers hoping to evade capture. When the detective knocks their balls away the robbers are sent to jail—a designated area in one corner of the grid. Once a person loses his ball, he must remain in jail until the end of the game. (He might practice his juggling while he's in there.)

Down to the final two players, the game becomes a one-on-one face-off between the crusading detective and the lone remaining dribbler, who tries to juke him out and make it to the designated jail area while retaining his dribble. The coach may embellish this drama by counting down from twenty-five, forcing the dribbler to make his move within this space of time. If the dribbler retains control of his ball and succeeds in reaching his captured mates, the game starts over, with a new person as detective.

THE CHAIN GAME

Players: 2 teams of 2
Area: Soccer field
Equipment: Traffic cones, 1 soccer ball for each player
Level of Difficulty: Advanced

The Chain Game is a tag game with a ball. To start, play within a coned-off area—say, ten feet by twelve feet. The less skilled the players, the more space they'll need.

Only two pairs can play at a time, but it is an easy thing to set up many games side by side. One team holds hands. They run and dodge and jump to avoid being hit by the ball kicked at them by the two players on the other team. The players with the ball pass and move and communicate. As soon as they score a hit on the other team, the two teams reverse roles. The team that formerly possessed the ball holds hands and starts running, while the other pair tries to hit them.

To make the game more difficult, and to ensure that nobody gets walloped too quickly, each player on the team with the ball must make three "touches" apiece before he can kick. (There can be fewer touches depending on the ages and skills of the players.) A touch is making contact with the ball with a part of the body, such as bouncing it against a knee or the head. If the team with the ball takes a shot and misses, each player must again make his three touches apiece. But if they hit, they grab hands and scamper away and the other duo immediately assumes control of the ball and begins their touches.

The Chain Game is a fast-paced, nearly nonstop way to improve teamwork and help teach youngsters to move with and without the ball.

Through the Legs

Players: 2
Area: Portion of soccer field
Equipment: Soccer ball
Level of Difficulty: Advanced

One person is the dribbler in Through the Legs. He stands with his back to his partner, who softly rolls or kicks a ball through the dribbler's legs and calls out a number from one to six. This signifies the number of "touches" the dribbler must make as he returns the ball back to the point of origin. If three is called, for example, the dribbler must maneuver the ball forward with two deft kicks. For his third touch, he must bring the ball back to the place where he started in front of his partner. The ball must be brought to a stop and under control, with the dribbler's foot resting on top of it. The final touch is a kind of presentation; the dribbler has made the requisite number of touches and everything is under control.

The dribbler needs to exercise judgment in addition to skill. If his partner has indicated six touches, the dribbler must judge the distance he has to cover even as he is quickly moving his feet. A partner can mix things up by tossing the ball over the dribbler's head to start the game, or to the left or right of his body—not just through the legs. He may even want to call out the touch number at the very last second, just before the dribbler is about to reach the ball. Obviously, after the dribbler has had his share of chances, the two should change positions.

Lose the Caboose

Players: Groups of 4 or 5
Area: Open field
Equipment: 1 soccer ball for each player
Level of Difficulty: Advanced

In this fast-moving dribbling game, the first player in the group is dubbed the engine and the last is the caboose. The engine leads the others around the field in a serpentine fashion, now slowly, now quickly, turning left here, veering right there. Everybody dribbles a ball and tries to keep up with the engine, which tries to shake the caboose loose from the rest of the cars. If the engine does shake the caboose loose, the caboose is out of the game.

But fair's fair. The engine cannot suddenly "jump" the tracks with a haphazard move or curl the line of players back onto itself. Its movements should be flowing and consistent. The engine will want to be fair because before long a coach may call out "Switch!" and make it change roles with the caboose. At that point the line starts moving in the opposite direction with the former caboose now in the lead and the one-time engine taking up the rear, desperate to hang on.

For an interesting variation, at the time of a switch, make the caboose dribble to the front of the line while the engine stays in place and everybody is still moving. This pushes all the players back one and lets a new player become the caboose.

EMBO

Players: Groups of 5 or 6
Area: Soccer field
Equipment: 1 soccer ball per group, 1 goal
Level of Difficulty: Advanced

EMBO stands for "Everybody Must Bend Over." However, to spell it out completely, it would be "Everybody Must Bend Over and Get Their Butts Thumped by a Soccer Ball."

EMBO is like the famous basketball game Horse. Players receive letters for miscues, and the first one to spell out E-M-B-O must suffer the consequences. Each person keeps track of his or her letters. EMBO is basically a juggling game. Five or six players stand in a loose circle and pass the ball around. No using the hands, of course; if someone does, he receives a letter. The first miscue earns that person an E, the second an M, and so forth. The players juggle the ball among themselves, using their feet, thighs, ankles, shoulders, chest, and head—anything to keep the ball from hitting the ground. If someone drops the ball or makes a pass to another person that is deemed unplayable, he earns a letter.

How the ball travels around the circle can vary. On the first time around, each player may make one touch before passing. On the second time, he makes two; on the third, three, etc. A touch is defined as one contact with the body. With five players in the group, the progression builds to five touches and then makes a stepped descent to one touch around the circle again.

Along the way the players are collecting letters for dropped balls, wayward passes, poor effort, and the like. The first to receive all four letters (EMBO) is the person who must bend over. He takes up this stance—butt facing outward—in front of the soccer net, while the others set up for a free kick at him a safe distance away. They try to rocket the ball squarely onto the fellow's derriere, and although they almost never do, they receive great amusement in trying. Each person is entitled to one kick apiece, but if the target flinches or moves in any way, everyone gets another go at him.

No sensible kicker ever tries to bash the ball too hard though, because of an inspired EMBO rule. If, in his zeal to make a direct hit, one player kicks so hard that the ball goes wide or flies above the net, he must change places with his intended target and take his lumps himself.

BACK DOOR

Players: 2 teams of 4 or more
Area: Shortened soccer field
Equipment: 1 soccer ball, 2 goals
Level of Difficulty: Advanced

Back Door should be played on a shortened field. Bring the goals in—even as close as eighteen yards apart, the length of the penalty box. This will create more rallies and give players more touches of the ball.

There are no goalies in Back Door, and points are scored—here's the twist—from behind the goal. Players must take the ball past the goal and shoot it back into the goal to score. But they must temper their enthusiasm with good judgment, for if they shoot wildly and miss, the ball will now be rolling in the direction of the opposite goal, giving the other team a golden opportunity for a fast break. Back Door provides a surprisingly tough workout because, although the field is smaller than regulation, the game moves quickly and in being forced to go behind the goal players run much more than usual.

FOUR-GOAL

Players: 2 teams of 5
Area: Soccer field
Equipment: 4 goals, lots of soccer balls
Level of Difficulty: Advanced

Four-Goal requires four goals on the field—two in the customary positions, two across from each other along the middle of the sidelines. The field should be shortened according to the age and abilities of the participants.

Teams can shoot for any goal they choose. Players play defense, but there are no goalies. After a team scores, that goal becomes off limits until someone makes another score somewhere else. This rule creates considerable confusion, for in their rush to hit the ball into the net and score points for their team the players often forget which goal is closed. If a player shoots into a prohibited goal, his or her team loses a point. Whether a person should defend a goal or take the ball himself and shoot it into a goal, is completely up to him.

Only one goal is off limits at any one time, but that goal is constantly shifting. The coach adds to the confusion by tossing balls onto the field of play, often in front of the prohibited net. A game of Four-Goal may have two or three balls going at the same time. If someone kicks out of bounds, don't give chase; just throw in another ball. The players keep right on going, kicking for a goal that may or may not be open, as best as they can recall.

Other ways to play: With the four goals set up in this fashion, play soccer with each team protecting two goals. Each team should have to defend an end goal and a sideline goal. If a player scores in either of the two goals, that is a point for his or her side. Again, no goalies.

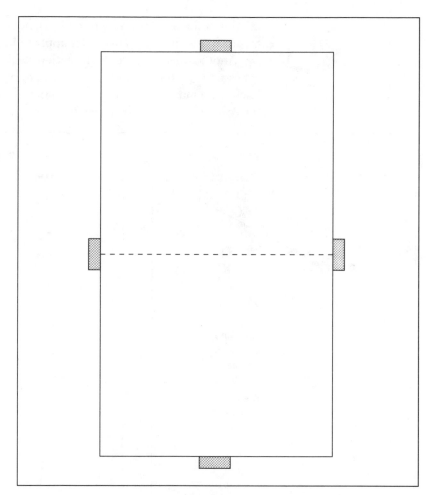

FOUR - GOAL

Wingers Game

Players: 10–20
Area: Soccer field
Equipment: Soccer ball,
2 goals, traffic
cones (optional)
Level of Difficulty:
Advanced

Wingers Game places the more advanced players in a game situation, but the rules restrict the type of game they can play, encouraging them to pass more and take the ball down the side of the field rather than always jamming into the middle.

Each corner of the field is numbered—1, 2, 3, and 4. At these corners are marked-off rectangular zones where the attacking teams must pass before they can take a shot on goal. For instance, the Blues are pushing the ball into the end of the field with corners 3 and 4. The coach stipulates that they must pass first into 3, then 4, before going for the goal. The coach also has the right—coaches always do—to change his mind. On the next time down the field, he may order the Blues to pass first into 4, then 3. The same rules apply to Blues' opponents, of course.

Another method to force the action away from the center is to place cones along both sides of the field and station players behind these cones. Each team must pass a specified number of times to the person behind the cones as it moves down the field toward its goal.

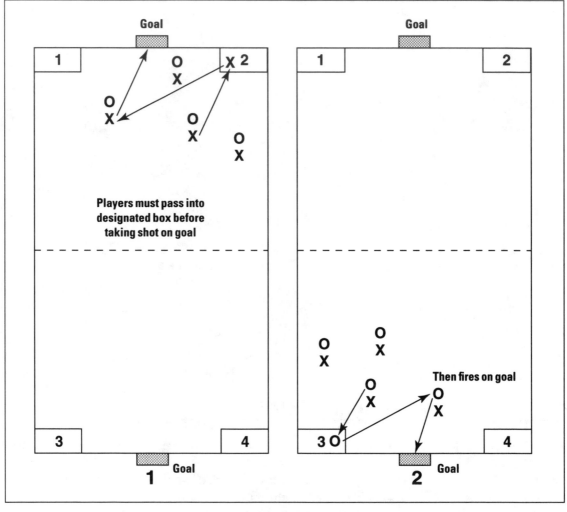

WINGERS GAME

HANDBALL SOCCER

Players: 2 teams of 7
Area: Gym
Equipment: Playground ball, 2 indoor soccer goals
Level of Difficulty: Advanced

Handball Soccer is a cross between Indoor Soccer (page 125) and Team Handball (page 191). Invented by John Tsubota, a California middle school P.E. teacher, it is a physical game that helps youngsters blow off steam on a a rainy day.

When the ball is on the floor, the game moves like soccer; it's a foot game. But players can handle the ball as well—not by simply picking it up, but by boosting it up with their feet (or other body parts). Once a player has the ball in his hands he can throw it to his teammates advancing down the floor. Air dribbling—passing to yourself to advance the ball—is permitted, one per possession, and a player may take three steps when he shoots. If the ball rolls on the floor, the game returns to soccer. As in Indoor Soccer, the walls are in play; a player can kick the ball off the wall and catch it in his hands.

Play Handball Soccer in a gym using the smaller indoor soccer goals. Set the goals up on the baseline under the basketball rims. The game begins with a face-off at center court. Each team lines up on its own side to start; after the face-off the players stream freely up and down the court.

Players can score either by kicking or by throwing. Like Team Handball, an arc around the goal—the 3-point line on a basketball court—functions as a forbidden area for shooters. All *throwing* shots on goal must take place outside that line. Players may kick balls a la soccer from inside the line, however. Once the goalie puts his foot on the ball, all the players must back off. Otherwise things can get a little dicey, with everybody kicking all at once. All goals count for 1 point.

Players who show an inclination to hang around the net and cherrypick for easy goals should be discouraged. Nevertheless, strict enforcement of offsides rules is not in keeping with the kinetic, energetic vitality of Handball Soccer. Body checking is likewise not allowed, but anyone who expects young boys not to have some degree of physical contact when playing this game understands neither boys nor how they play games.

SPEEDBALL

Players: 12–20
Area: Soccer field
Equipment: Soccer ball
Level of Difficulty:
    Advanced

Speedball brings the hands into soccer. Because it allows the use of the hands, it is not a true soccer game. Nevertheless, it is great fun and it does help develop many soccer skills. Players can touch the ball with their hands, although (as in Handball Soccer) they cannot simply grab it up off the ground but must lift the ball up with their feet, or rebound it off their body or someone else's body. Once they secure possession of the ball, they may pass it on to a teammate. They may air dribble once a possession.

The element of the pass energizes the game considerably, and Speedball certainly deserves its monicker. Apart from the use of the hands, and the rules of scoring, Speedball resembles soccer in all important aspects. There are three ways to score in Speedball: an old-fashioned football-style dropkick over the goal (3 points), an ordinary kicking goal into the net (2 points), and a passing goal (1 point). But the passing goal comes with qualifications. Players cannot score by throwing the ball into the net; the passing goal is earned by a simple pass into a designated area in front of the goalie. However, most young players tend to ignore this option entirely. Not only because it is only worth 1 point, but because it is far less satisfying than the other two methods. Youth will be served, and when they can go for the glory of kicking the ball into—or over—the net, they will do it in almost every case.

TWELVE

SWIMMING AND DIVING

O f all the major sports covered in this book, swimming is unique in that it does not have a ball at the center of it. It takes place in a different medium, and it requires more of a commitment to physical conditioning than many ball sports. Breath control and stamina are as important in swimming as proper stroke technique.

Beginning swimmers and those who are just learning must feel comfortable in the water. This early goal of swim instruction should not be forgotten as children progress into more advanced age-group competition. Burnout is a problem in all sports, but perhaps especially so in swimming. Young people whose bodies are still developing often swim so much that they exhaust themselves mentally and physically. They lose interest and motivation, and many quit in rebellion. Playing a game in the pool or staging a wacky relay race at the end of a workout will help relieve the monotony and keep spirits high, giving those earnest and dedicated young athletes a healthy way to blow off some steam. Many of these games are also suitable for backyard pools, lakes, and streams.

TAG IN A POOL

Players: 3 or more
Area: Swimming pool
Equipment: None
(except for
swimsuits, of
course)
Level of Difficulty: Easy

Nowadays, children take lessons to learn how to swim. In an earlier time, many children learned to swim by playing tag in a pool. They ran around the pool chased by the It person. When they reached a corner, however, they had to go in the water. Those were the rules: They could not pass a corner of the pool without going in. They dove in, swam underwater, ran or churned strokes to evade their pursuer. If they wished they could get out again, but when they reached a corner, in they went once more. And gradually they got stronger and stronger in the water.

Now, however, unless it's a backyard pool or special circumstances, for safety reasons lifeguards prohibit people from running on the concrete decks of swimming pools. It's too dangerous; a person could slip and fall. But while the older version of the game may be gone for good, Tag in a Pool remains as vibrant as ever. Go to any pool and there will be children darting and dodging in high-spirited games of water tag. A child need not know how to swim to play tag and enjoy it, and without realizing it these simple games may be his first steps in losing his fear of water and becoming a swimmer.

PORPOISE TAG

Players: Unlimited
Area: Swimming pool
Equipment: None
Level of Difficulty: Easy

Porpoise Tag is one of the seemingly endless variety of tag games that children can play in a pool. In order to make a tag in this game, a person must dive down under the water and come back again, mimicking the actions of a porpoise or dolphin. A tag can only be made in this way.

Porpoise Tag is a shallow-water game. One person can be It and tag someone, who in turn becomes It. Or the taggers could unite and chase after all the rest until all have been captured. The what of Porpoise Tag is not as important as the how. The game teaches breath control and is particularly good in helping beginning swimmers get over their fear of going underwater.

Other ways to play: In Underwater Tag, the person who's It swims underwater to catch his or her prey. The It person can only tag another person while underwater.

FRISBEE CATCH

Players: 2–3
Area: Swimming pool
Equipment: Frisbee
Level of Difficulty: Easy

For many children, getting their head wet is the biggest early obstacle in learning how to swim. Once they get over that barrier—once they feel comfortable about dipping their head under water, coming up for air, and dipping down again—they've got it made. Their fears about the water vanish, and they are now ready to learn how to carve strokes in the water.

Frisbee Catch is a simple way to help break down this barrier. Catch with a Nerf football or baseball also works. Kids can really feel like a hero when they play catch in a pool. They can launch themselves in the air, extend themselves out like a third-baseman diving for a ball hit down the line, and create a big splash when they land. They can make still more spectacular catches by sliding down a slide or jumping off the diving board.

CANNONBALL CONTEST

Players: Unlimited
Area: Diving pool or deep end of swimming pool
Equipment: Diving board
Level of Difficulty: Easy–Moderate

This is a game of pure fun. Everybody knows how to do a cannonball, right? Just get as much elevation as possible, curl the knees up, and KERSPLASH! Biggest splash wins.

MARCO POLO

Players: Unlimited
Area: Swimming pool
Equipment: None
Level of Difficulty: Moderate

This most popular of all swimming games owes its name to the Venetian explorer of the late 1200s and early 1300s whose travels to China, India, and other parts of Asia helped introduce the "mysterious Orient" to Western Europe. Legend says that Marco Polo did not know where he was going when he first set out on his travels—hence the game's name.

One swimmer begins as Marco. He pretends that he is blind and closes his eyes as he journeys about the pool looking for someone to tag. Whenever he chooses he calls out "Marco!" to which the others in the game must respond "Polo!" The other swimmers can stay still or make noise or go underwater. But when Marco calls for his bearings, they must cooperate. These clues should help Marco find a victim, who takes over as the new Marco.

It must be anticipated that, like their parents at income tax time, children will cheat. It is a rare Marco indeed who actually does keep his eyes closed. If he does play fair, he is often subjected to taunting and jeering from the other players evading his tag—those same players who peeked when they were Marco. Nonetheless, Marco Polo would never have attained such time-tested popularity if it weren't also lots of good fun.

CRAZY DIVE CONTEST

Players: Unlimited
Area: Diving pool or deep end of swimming pool
Equipment: Diving board
Level of Difficulty: Moderate

This is another diving game just for the fun of it. It may also help young divers loosen up and relax. Crazy Diving rewards not mere bulk or splash power as in the Cannonball Contest, but creative expressions of artistic value. Whoever stages the goofiest mid-air exhibition wins. Contestants are judged by a jury of their peers.

The consolation prize in this event is known as the Weanie. Undoubtedly contestants will try many types of dives, flirting precariously with the belly flop. Anyone who actually does a belly flop, slamming the water with his or her stomach, wins the Weanie.

SHARKS AND MINNOWS

Players: Unlimited
Area: Swimming pool
Equipment: None
Level of Difficulty: Moderate

The easy way to play Sharks and Minnows—another classic swimming game—is as a touch game. One person is the shark, the others are minnows. The minnows start at one end of the pool, swimming underwater to reach the opposite wall. There, the shark lies in wait. If the shark touches one of the minnows before it reaches the wall, the minnow turns into a shark too. Then the minnows swim back to the other end, with the sharks trying to catch them. Over time the sharks multiply and gobble up all the minnows.

But this version of Sharks and Minnows is not without drawbacks. Inevitably, there are arguments of the "I-touched-you!" "No-you-didn't!" variety. One way to avoid this is to toughen up the requirements for the sharks. Rather than a simple touch, in order to be caught a minnow must be brought to the surface and forced to breathe. This means that a smaller shark may be unable to subdue a bigger and more powerful minnow all by himself and must enlist recruits. The next time down the pool, he and a few of his toothy comrades can pounce on that oversized minnow and drag him up to the surface before he reaches the wall.

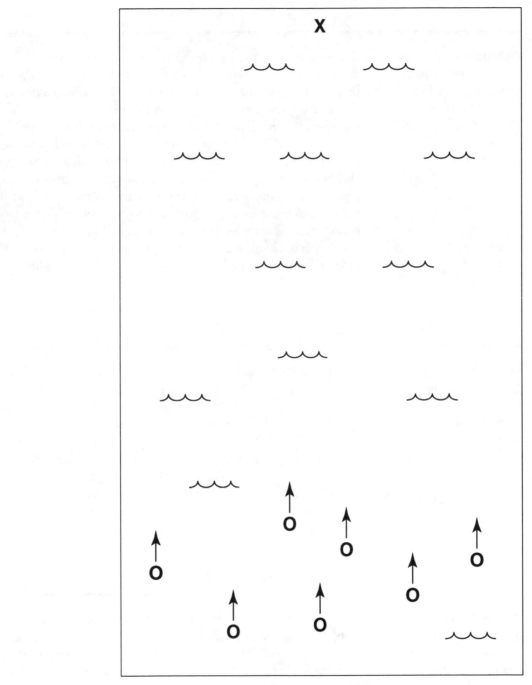

SHARKS AND MINNOWS

BARNACLE

Players: 2
Area: Swimming pool
Equipment: None
Level of Difficulty:
    Moderate–advanced

Barnacle is a game for brothers, sisters, close friends, even a parent and child. Play Barnacle in medium-shallow water, so that both participants can stand easily on the bottom. A barnacle is a tiny sea animal that attaches itself to the hulls of ships or rocks—and that is what the players in this game do: Attach themselves to each other.

More precisely, one player—the barnacle—attaches himself, while the other tries to get free. To extricate himself from the barnacle's clutches he dives, twists, spins, rolls, holds his breath underwater, pushes, pulls, jumps, and whatever else he can manage to do. The barnacle, meanwhile, holds on for dear life. A person is not free of the barnacle unless completely unstuck, with no body contact. Even if only one desperate, lunging claw of the barnacle is hanging to the ankle of the other, he is still attached, and the rolling, splashing, laughing game goes on.

JUMP OR DIVE!

Players: Unlimited
Area: Diving pool
Equipment: Diving board
Level of Difficulty:
    Moderate–advanced

One player stands on the diving board, another stands on the pool deck. The one on the board takes several fast steps forward and, at the very last instant, just before takeoff, in that millisecond where the board disappears into thin air, the one on the ground yells, "Jump!" Or he yells "Dive!" Whatever he yells, the person on the board must respond instantly and do it. In all likelihood there will be a group of youngsters waiting impatiently behind the one on the board and they will follow behind him in rapid-fire fashion, either jumping or diving per the shouted instructions. Prudence dictates that Jump or Dive! should be played on the one-meter board, not the three-meter board.

WACKY RELAY RACES

Players: Teams of 4
Area: 25-yard swimming
    pool
Equipment: None
Level of Difficulty:
    Moderate–advanced

If Doctor Seuss had been a swimmer, he would have enjoyed Wacky Relay Races. Wacky Relay Races are a green eggs and ham kind of thing. They're a thing that a Zizzer-Zazzer-Zuzz would appreciate, or a Hakken-Krak, or The Cat in the Hat, if the Cat did not mind getting his Hat wet.

No one swims their relay legs in an ordinary way. Swimmers must swim the butterfly on their back, flinging their arms about in a most strange and amusing fashion. For the freestyle, they swim the crawl stroke using the dolphin kick of the butterfly. For the breaststroke leg, they use the flutter kick of the freestyle while breaststroking with their arms. And, on the backstroke, they kick like a breaststroker and use the butterfly stroke while scooting backward on their back.

Wacky Relay Races require great coordination, and the strokes can be altered—freestyle stroke and breaststroke kick? butterfly kick on the back?—to suit the whim of the coaches and swimmers. Doctor Seuss would approve.

Swim Fin Water Polo

Players: 2 teams of 5 or more, with 1 goalie

Area: Swimming pool

Equipment: Swim fins for each player, soccer ball, water polo goal

Level of Difficulty: Moderate–advanced

The Olympic sport of Water Polo is a demanding game that is probably beyond the skills and physical capacities of most preteens. But put flippers on their feet and it's a whole new ballgame.

Unlike regulation Water Polo, which uses the entire pool, Swim Fin Water Polo only takes place in a portion of it. "Half-court" water polo cuts down on the amount of swimming a person must do, although there will still be plenty of that. Players are organized on teams. Each team tries to throw the ball into the goal and score points. After a shot on goal, the ball must be cleared beyond a certain point; the backstroke flags are an obvious marker. Both teams must swim out to the flags when the ball is cleared. This opens up the possibility for a fast break even though the game is only half-court. If one team hustles to clear the ball before the other team has had time to set up its defense, it may have a clear shot on goal.

Scoring in Swim Fin Water Polo is the same as in the regulation game—1 point per goal. The attacking team closes in on the goal, passing the ball crisply around the perimeter until one person rises up and fires a lighting bolt into the net. Since this is a half-court game, the goalie must play for both teams. This would be a good role for a coach or parent, someone who can be objective and who doesn't care who wins. A heavier ball such as a soccer ball is recommended in this game.

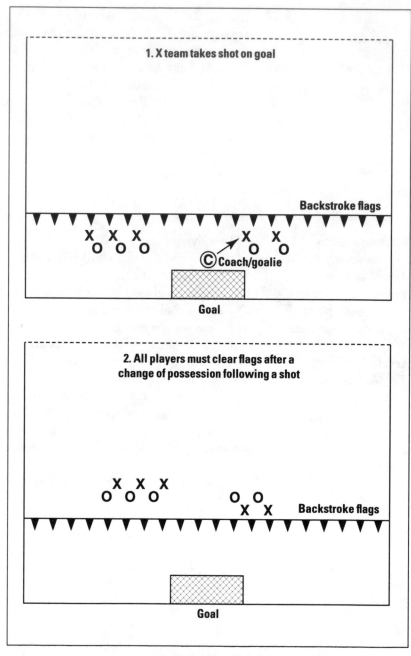

SWIM FIN WATER POLO

Inner Tube Water Polo

Players: 2 teams of 5
apiece

Area: Swimming pool

Equipment: 1 inner tube
for each player,
water polo ball,
water polo goals

Level of Difficulty:
Advanced

In Inner Tube Water Polo, each player has a vessel to paddle. They paddle this way and that, kicking up lots of spray, and sometimes somebody even scores a goal.

Older players—say, ten years and above—will likely need a truck tire tube. Younger children can get by with just a car tube. While the backward propulsion methods of many of the players may appear comical to the neutral observer, Inner Tube Water Polo has its own set of rules and regulations just like any of the more serious games. If a person gets out of his tube, he cannot touch the ball. He can only carry the ball when he is inside his tube. However, it is okay if he takes the ball out of his tube and lets it ride the current next to him while he stays afloat. In fact, when he is doing this he cannot be touched or otherwise manhandled by the other players.

Now if a person is carrying the ball while in his tube and advancing toward the goal, he can be intercepted by the opposition. It is quite within the rules for a defender to flip the ball carrier into the water by (a) pushing down hard on one side of the tube, or (b) grabbing the person, putting a foot on the tube, and pulling him over. Once the ball carrier is out of his tube, remember, he cannot advance the ball. This should enable the person still in his tube to scoop the ball up and start paddling back in the other direction.

Though tipping people over and knocking them out of their tubes is an integral part of the game, roughhouse tactics are certainly discouraged. If a person commits five fouls, he must relinquish his tube to the referee and chill out on the pool deck. Nor can players without the ball be clotheslined when the referee isn't looking.

Players may not bring the ball all the way into the net and score. They must unload from outside the shooting line five meters from the goal. A team might consist of four players and one goalie, including participants from both sexes.

Chase Down

Players: Unlimited
Area: Swimming pool
with 6 lanes, lane
ropes
Equipment: None
Level of Difficulty:
Advanced

Chase Down is a workout game. It can motivate fast swimmers into going faster and give slow swimmers the impetus to pick up speed.

Rope off six lanes. The swimmers start from Lane One. They swim up Lane One and back Lane Two, up Lane Three and back Lane Four, up Lane Five and back to the finish line at the wall of Lane Six. The slower swimmers get the gun first, going off in stages according to their abilities. Their mission is to not get caught from behind. The faster swimmers go out in stages behind them with the goal of catching and passing the ones in front of them.

But these faster swimmers cannot simply climb over bodies as they churn toward the Lane Six wall. If they accidentally touch someone while passing, they must stop to wait until one person passes them. After they themselves are humbled in this fashion, they can resume their all-out pursuit.

Shotgun Relays

Players: Relay teams
Area: Swimming pool,
lane ropes
Equipment: None
Level of Difficulty:
Advanced

Shotgun Relays is a team variation of Chase Down. The same guiding principle applies: The slower swimmers get a lead, the faster ones try to reel them in. However, in this race each team stays in its own lane.

One relay team may get a ten-second lead before another team is allowed to take off. This team may in turn get a five-second lead over the faster team starting behind it. Like Chase Down, a staggered relay of this kind can be demoralizing to the slower swimmers if it is not managed well. This is where the skill of the coach comes in. He or she should have a solid sense of the abilities of the swimmers and how much time to allow between groups. The race should really be a sprint to the finish. As they strain to reach the wall both the slower and faster swimmers should feel in their pounding hearts that they really *can* get there first.

Underwater Relays

Players: Unlimited
Area: Swimming pool
Equipment: None
Level of Difficulty:
Advanced

Underwater Relays are yet another fun approach to relays. Swimmers must swim the length of the pool underwater. They take a racing start and use an underwater frog kick. It might be wise to station a referee underwater at the wall to make sure that everyone indeed touches before their teammates take off. Swimmers cannot touch the

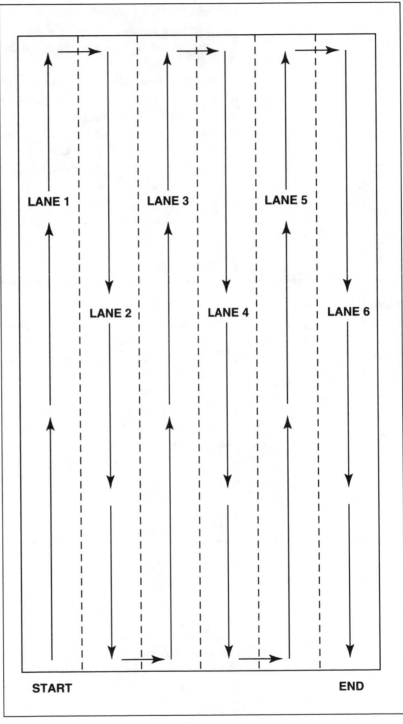

CHASE DOWN

bottom of the pool with their feet. Some clever swimmers may try to get an advantage by pushing off the bottom and catapulting themselves forward, so the underwater referee should try to keep an eye out for that too.

Other ways to play: Get the coach involved! Suppose the team wants to raise some money to travel to an upcoming meet. For every underwater lap the coach swims, the parents or the team members themselves agree to chip in $1 (or whatever). The rules may stipulate that the coach can breathe at the wall after twenty-five yards underwater or, if he has Aqua-lungs, see how many laps he can do consecutively without breathing. Children and parents alike will get a kick out of seeing the coach bust his lungs for the team.

CATCHUP

Players: Teams of 4
Area: Swimming pool
Equipment: None
Level of Difficulty:
   Advanced

Catchup splits each team in half—two swimmers per team on one side of the pool, two swimmers on the other side. When the whistle blows the first swimmer on one side swims a twenty-five-yard sprint to the wall, while the first swimmer on the opposing team, *starting from the other side,* does the same. The two are swimming against each other but going in opposite directions.

The object is for one team to catch the other. It makes for a terrific workout, each kid doing an all-out freestyle sprint, resting while her teammates are in the water, then going again. A Catchup race ends when one team makes up the stagger and catches the other.

MORE RELAY IDEAS

Players: Unlimited
Area: Swimming pool
Equipment: None
Level of Difficulty:
   Advanced

Tee-Shirt Relays:
Swimmers swim in a tee shirt that they pass off to the next person after finishing their leg. The tee shirt is the great equalizer; it really sticks. The secret of success lies in taking it off in the water; if the swimmer does that, she can make the exchange fairly quickly. If she doesn't, she's sunk.

Feet-First Relays:
Whether they lie on their back facing forward, or on their stomach facing backward, the contestants must propel themselves in the water with their feet first.

One-Arm Relays:

Only one arm allowed. An amusing variation: One arm, one leg.

Corkscrew Relays:

Swim one arm-stroke of freestyle, roll onto the back and over, swim another freestyle stroke, roll onto the back, etc. Swimmers get twisted up as they roll around the lanes.

THIRTEEN

TENNIS

Consistency is usually the biggest challenge for young tennis players. Many youngsters try to kill the ball, hoping to hit it hard and straight like they see the professionals do on TV. Helping players "unlearn" this tendency, while gaining consistency and control, is a major goal of early tennis instruction. Youngsters should learn the benefits of playing percentage tennis—of serving and hitting to spots, and hitting with a purpose. They should know how to set up points and be aware of the basic elements of tennis strategy, particularly in doubles.

The annals of tennis are filled with the stories of tennis wunderkinds, gifted young prodigies who rose to stardom and attained Wimbledon titles while still only teenagers. Unfortunately, this has caused some overstriving parents and coaches to push their young tennis players in an extreme and unhealthy manner. Caring individuals should ever be on the guard against this, remembering always to mix in a little fun and games with the drills.

Anything Goes

Players: 4–8
Area: Tennis court
Equipment: Tennis rackets, extra balls
Level of Difficulty: Easy

Anything Goes is ideal for young players who are just learning the game. It is typically a doubles game, but there's no reason why four (or even more) players can't play on each side of the court. As the title suggests, anything goes.

A ball may bounce once, twice, or one hundred times on a side. It may bounce off the court, over the fence, and down the street. As long as it keeps bouncing, the ball remains alive and in play. After running it down, a player may scoop it off the ground with the racket and "bubble" it—bounce it repeatedly off the strings—back to the court. Then he or she can knock it over the net, resuming the point in progress. This is all allowed.

The point is over when a ball starts to roll. Until then, players can scoop it up with their rackets and continue playing. The one mild restriction in Anything Goes is that the first hit over the net must land fair. Keeping score is optional and probably counter-productive, at that.

Mini-Tennis (Dinkum)

Players: 4
Area: Tennis court
Equipment: Tennis rackets, balls
Level of Difficulty: Easy

Mini-Tennis brings the court down to match the size of the players. Two play singles on one half of the court, two play on the other half. They use only the service court. If they serve (some coaches may want to feed the ball in themselves), they serve from behind the service box. With the court effectively cut in half, young players have less to think about and can concentrate on improving their touch and control. Play to 4.

21 (Serving Game)

Players: 2 or 4
Area: Tennis court
Equipment: Tennis rackets, balls
Level of Difficulty: Easy

21 is a scoring game designed to help with serves and returns. Players play singles. If a player's first serve goes in, she earns 2 points. Second serve scores 1 point. All successful returns count for 1 point. Scoring is cumulative. So if the server gets her first serve in (2 points) and returns two shots during the point, she scores 4. Her opponent, returning the ball twice, earns 2. Both keep their points and go to the end of the line, allowing two more the chance to play. The first in the group to accumulate 21 points wins.

Around the World

Players: Unlimited
Area: Tennis court
Equipment: Tennis
 rackets, balls
Level of Difficulty:
 Easy–moderate

Around the World may be the most popular of all tennis games for young players. It moves quickly, and a spirit of joyful camaraderie often arises among the participants.

Two groups of players line up single file on opposite sides of the net. These groups will be hitting back and forth to one another, rotating between lines as they do. Depending on the abilities of the players, a coach may want to feed the ball in. One person hits, then runs to his or her right, circling around the net to the end of the opposite line. As this person leaves, a new player steps forward ready to hit. The other side does the same—hitting and then crossing around to the opposite side of the court. Each person hits and runs, hits and runs. As soon as children are old enough to hit the ball over the net, they can play this fun, fast-paced classic.

King or Queen of the Mountain

Players: Unlimited
Area: Tennis court
Equipment: Tennis
 rackets, balls
Level of Difficulty:
 Easy–moderate

Another classic tennis game, King or Queen of the Mountain is a play-until-you-lose singles contest. Let's say a boy begins as king. He plays a one-point match against a challenger. If he wins, he remains king and plays the next contender for the throne waiting in line. If the challenger wins, she becomes queen and earns the right to take on all comers until she herself is usurped. Players should line up on both sides of the court so that when one person loses, a new person can quickly jump in. Serve is optional.

Target Practice

Players: Unlimited
Area: Tennis court
Equipment: Tennis
 rackets, extra balls
Level of Difficulty:
 Easy–moderate

Young players should learn to serve to their opponent's weakness. Target Practice will encourage them to serve with a specific intent in mind beyond just getting the ball in.

Set up four balls—three on the bottom, one on top—at the far corners of the service boxes. Place the balls just inside the lines, not on them. Junior sharpshooters get four serves per turn—one per target—to see how many piles of balls they can scatter.

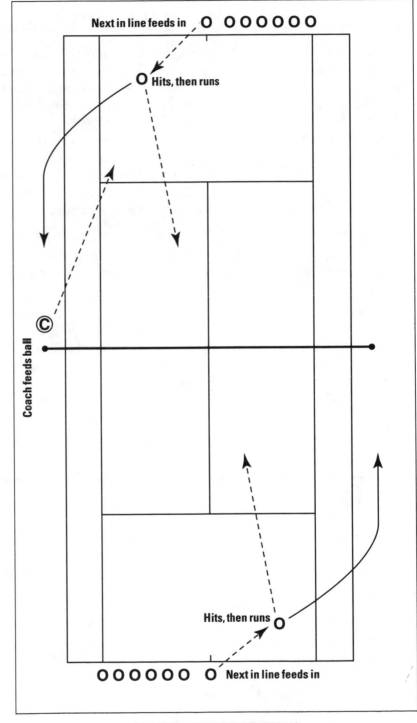

AROUND THE WORLD (TENNIS)

SERVE AND RETURN

Players: 2 or 4
Area: Tennis court
Equipment: Tennis rackets, balls
Level of Difficulty: Easy–moderate

The object of tennis usually is to score points and win—but not in this game. The idea behind Serve and Return is *not* to hit winners (that is, balls that cannot be returned); in fact, the loser is the one who hits the ball last, but prevents the rally from continuing by not making his hit easily returnable.

Play singles or doubles, or split the court in two and let two players play on one half and two on the other half. Indeed, this latter arrangement is preferable, because it makes it easier for young players to control the ball. Serve and Return teaches consistency, keeping the ball under control, and hitting with a purpose.

31

Players: 2 or 4
Area: Tennis court
Equipment: Tennis rackets, balls
Level of Difficulty: Easy–moderate

31 teaches through a different sort of scoring system than the usual. The person who wins the point, scores 2 points. If in doing so he hits a winner—the opponent doesn't touch the ball—he scores 3 points. But a person can lose the point and still score, if he hits long. A ball that goes over the baseline counts 1 point for the person who hit it. Meanwhile, if a person hits the ball into the net, he is penalized 2 points. The purpose of this scoring system is to get young players to really clear the net and hit deep. Game is to 31. No serve.

VOLLEY TO VOLLEY

Players: 2 or 4
Area: Tennis court
Equipment: Tennis rackets, balls
Level of Difficulty: Moderate

Volley to Volley is just what its name implies. Shorten the court; eliminate the serve. Players stand inside the service box hitting forehands to forehands, backhands to backhands, and cross-court shots of forehand to backhand, backhand to forehand. Players quickly learn that in this game, nice 'n' easy does it. The ball should only touch the racket strings, never the ground, and the twosome that accomplishes the most volleys in a row wins.

21 (Return Game)

Players: 2 or 4
Area: Tennis court
Equipment: Tennis rackets, balls
Level of Difficulty: Moderate

This more advanced version of 21 eliminates the serve. A coach or supervisor feeds the ball into play, and the game proceeds from there. Players play singles. All successful returns count for 1 point. But no scoring can take place until both players have hit at least once. If there are lots of players involved, two people play a point and then go to the end of the line, allowing others the chance to play. The winner is the one who reaches 21 first.

Net Ball

Players: 2
Area: Tennis court
Equipment: Tennis rackets, balls
Level of Difficulty: Moderate–advanced

Net Ball does away with the conventional way to begin a point and brings the two players up to the net. Every point starts at the net. One player balances the ball on the net tape and lets it drop. The other must react to it and get it back over with a drop shot return, or a lob over the head, or some other clever response. They then play the point out. When the point is over they return to the net and start over. Rather than standing back at the baseline and banging away, as many younger players are wont to do, Net Ball demands a refreshingly different kind of tennis from them.

Lob Ball

Players: 2
Area: Tennis court
Equipment: Tennis rackets, balls
Level of Difficulty: Moderate–advanced

Sorry, no passing shots allowed. In Lob Ball, only lobs and overheads will do. The game begins with a lob (a coach can feed the ball in from the side) to players at the baseline. When back at the baseline, they must hit lobs. When they move up to the net or service line, they must follow with an overhead. Lob Ball is a simple way to improve doubles skills and practice these difficult-to-do shots. For every successful lob or overhead, score one point. Game is to 10.

AUSTRALIAN TENNIS

Players: 3
Area: Tennis court
Equipment: Tennis
　rackets, balls
Level of Difficulty:
　Moderate–advanced

Stuck for a fourth? Australian Tennis offers a novel solution: two against one. The two play the doubles court, while the one plays the singles court. Rotate after four points. The first person to score 10 points on the singles side wins.

TRIPLES

Players: 6
Area: Tennis court
Equipment: Tennis
　rackets, balls
Level of Difficulty:
　Moderate–advanced

Triples is doubles plus two. It is a wild game that puts three players on each side of the court at the same time. People get shots at angles they don't normally see. The entire court is covered. Usually two people play the net while their partner handles the baseline.

PEPPER

Players: 2
Area: Tennis court
Equipment: Tennis
　rackets, balls
Level of Difficulty:
　Advanced

Pepper is big fun. Players try to hit their opponent's feet with the ball—or, at least, to make them jump like crazy.

The game takes place inside the service lines, on one half of the service court. Narrowing the court down gives the players more of a chance to pepper each other. The players cannot go behind the service line; indeed, they should be always closing in on the net. Older, more experienced players will do better at Pepper, because they will be more adept at keeping the ball low. The ball should always come low across the net. The person who pops it into the air becomes a sitting duck for a hard-placed volley aimed at his feet. Award prizes to anyone who actually succeeds in hitting an opponent's feet.

TWO-ON-TWO RUSH THE NET

Players: 4
Area: Tennis court
Equipment: Tennis
　rackets, balls
Level of Difficulty:
　Advanced

Most tennis instructors would agree that it is difficult to teach young people how to play doubles. Boys especially want to do it all, swinging their racket at everything that comes in their vicinity even if it clearly has their partner's name on it. Youngsters are generally blind to the strategy and beauty of doubles, of two people moving and hitting as one, and when something goes awry they tend to blame their partner—not a recipe for doubles success.

Two-on-Two Rush the Net will not teach young people maturity, but it will help their doubles game. It will encourage them to attack the net while working together as a team. Both teams start from the baseline. There is no serve, and a team can score only after each side handles at least one ball. The rule in this game is that both players must come to the net on a short ball. One player cannot hang back and let his partner do the work; it's all for one, and one for all. Play to 4, counting by ones.

AEROBIC DOUBLES

Players: 4
Area: Tennis court
Equipment: Tennis rackets, extra balls
Level of Difficulty: Advanced

Aerobic Doubles is a terrific running and high-energy game that begins with one team at the net. This team taps the ball into play. There is no serve; that would only slow things down. The tap-in must always land beyond the service line.

When the ball is in play, Aerobic Doubles is played like conventional doubles. But there are some big differences after a point is over. First of all, nobody fetches errant balls in Aerobic Doubles. When a point is over the winning team runs to the net and scoops up one of the balls that have been placed there. An abundance of balls should be placed at the base of the net, giving both sides plenty to choose from.

When the winning team rushes to the net, they must touch it together (togetherness is a must!), call out the score, and feed a ball into play as quickly as they can. They do not have to wait until the other team is ready; that's *their* responsibility. They can catch the other team napping by running hard and putting the ball rapidly into play. The other pair must respond or risk losing the point. The two teams then play the point in the doubles format. Up and back and all over the court they race, honing their doubles skills and working up a considerable sweat in the process. (Illustration is on next page.)

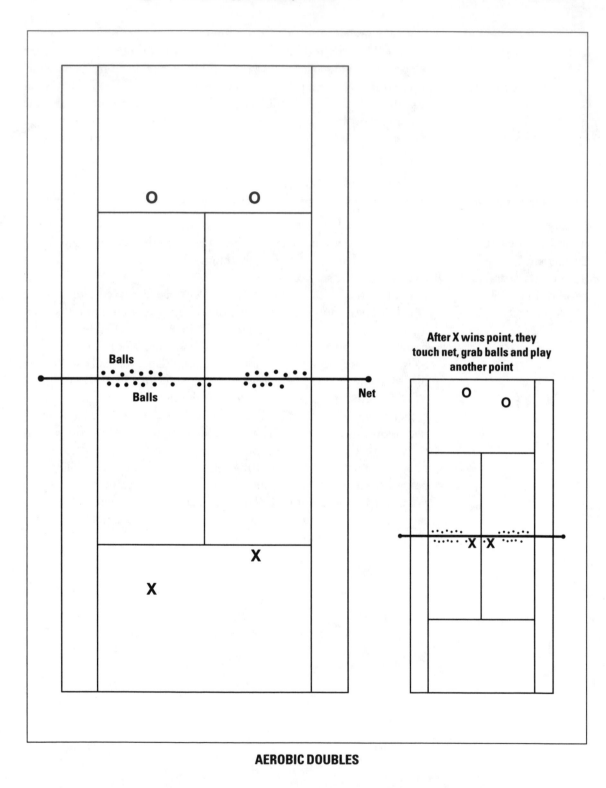

AEROBIC DOUBLES

FOURTEEN

VOLLEYBALL

Volleyball is a sport that stresses communication and teamwork. A net separates the opposing teams; unlike other team sports, there is no pushing and shoving between the two factions. The six players on a side jump and run and dive and step with balletic grace in an awfully small space, one of the smallest playing areas for any major sport. This puts a premium on working together, getting to know the other people on the team.

Volleyball is a misunderstood sport. Some people deride it as "unathletic." However, anyone who sees a volleyball coach stand on a ladder hammering balls over the net while the players dive across the floor trying to save them will quickly be disabused of this notion. Many people also think of volleyball as a game played only in southern California. While this area remains a volleyball hotbed, the game is now an Olympic sport played around the world. Some may also think of it as "a girl's sport." This is foolishness at its height. Boys as well as girls play this rigorous and demanding sport while demonstrating a fiery athleticism that other athletes can only admire.

BALLOON BALL

Players: 1
Area: Living room
Equipment: Balloon or
large beachball
Level of Difficulty: Easy

To a young pair of arms, a volleyball can be as hard as a rock. Playing with a balloon or a big and bouncy beachball is an easy way for young players to get started with the game. Nor does one need to go to the gym to play; given a tolerant set of parents, it can be done in the living room at home. In this way a youngster can combine watching television with the more useful pastime of Balloon Ball.

While seated in his or her favorite chair, the child "sets" the balloon into the air. Grabbing it and pushing it back up, the child forms a triangle underneath the balloon with the forefingers and thumbs of each hand touching. A densely packed volleyball can come down very hard and very fast. The beauty of a balloon is that it falls to earth at a deliciously slow rate, making it easy for the child to have success as well as creating a pleasant association—volleyball equals play—in the mind.

BALL-AWARENESS GAMES

Players: Unlimited
Area: Volleyball court
Equipment: Volleyballs
Level of Difficulty: Easy

Young people must learn to grow comfortable playing with a volleyball, much the same way that soccer players must grow comfortable with *their* ball. There are any number of ball-awareness drills that will work as games. Line the teams up in single file lines. Players must hand the ball over their head to the person behind them. When the ball gets to the end of the line, they reverse directions and hand the ball forward. The first team to go up and back wins. Or have them hand the ball around the side or between their legs.

A volleyball massage is another way to create ball awareness, in addition to being an excellent cool-down exercise after practice. One person lies on the floor while a teammate gives him a massage with the ball, rolling it all over the body. It feels real silly to the players, but it makes them feel more comfortable with the ball.

Other ways to play: Another method of developing ball awareness is to rapidly bounce a ball—not a balloon—on the floor—a gym floor, not the living room floor. Keep the hands together, bend the knees, get down over the ball, and bounce away. Still another way to develop soft hands is by bouncing the ball off a wall—again, at a gym or outside, not in the living room—at eye level or slightly above the head, using only the wrists and fingers, not the elbows. Give the ball a little push, catch it, and bounce it back. This can be played with friends: The person who bounces the ball most times without its falling wins a cold drink.

Newcomb

Players: 2 teams of 3 or more
Area: Volleyball court
Equipment: Volleyball
Level of Difficulty: Easy

Before players can bat the ball in the standard volleyball fashion, they might try catching and throwing it. The game is played just like regular volleyball, with games to 15 (or shorter, if preferred). But when the ball comes rocketing over the net players may catch it and, after tossing it among their teammates a maximum of three times, zing it back over the net with either one hand or two.

Gradually, as their skills improve, players can start to hit the ball. Each team catches, passes, and catches among themselves, but when the ball goes back over the net to the opposing team they must hit it.

Kling-On Tag

Players: Unlimited
Area: Half a volleyball court
Equipment: None
Level of Difficulty: Easy

In this fitness tag game for volleyball players, three is definitely a crowd. Everybody pairs off, linking arms. Players gather in a loose circle or within the half-court area. One person is designated as It, and his or her partner escapes by linking arms with another pair. The other pairs try to get away from the escapee. If the escapee succeeds in clinging onto some twosome, the person on the end is effectively cut loose. So the It or tagger chases after *him*. The only way this person can escape is by linking up with some other pair. When he does this, a new person is cut loose, and so it goes in this fun game that helps build team camaraderie.

Pac Man Tag

Players: 6–15
Area: Volleyball court
Equipment: None
Level of Difficulty: Easy

This is another fitness tag game that lets players run around and have a ball with their teammates. The interconnecting lines of a volleyball court form the playing area for this simple but fun game. Pac Man—the It person—must stay on the lines as he or she gives chase. So, too, must everyone else. Everybody must follow the lines; no jumping from line to line to avoid being tagged. If someone jumps off the line, just jump back on again!

PASSING

Players: 2
Area: Volleyball court or
open area
Equipment: Volleyball
Level of Difficulty:
Easy–moderate

Passing is to volleyball what catching and throwing are to baseball. It is the most fundamental skill in the game. And, like a baseball catch, it is a kind of dialog between two athletes with the focus of their conversation being a ball.

In the most elementary form of Passing, a person tosses the ball gently to her partner, who bumps or "digs" it out with her upturned forearms. The tosser catches it and throws it back, and her partner passes it to her again. Ten passes is a fair number of tries before the two switch roles, with the tosser getting her turn at bumping and digging.

As the players develop their skills, they forgo the toss and just pass the ball, digging and bumping to each other in turn. To be a good passer a person must get underneath the ball and, as the coaches say, "build a platform" with his or her arms—the forearms turned under and tucked firmly together.

Though Passing is as basic to volleyball as a game of Catch is to baseball, it is distinctly different in at least one major regard: Whereas in Catch the players are mostly stationary targets, with the spheroid zipping between them, this is most decidedly not the case in Passing. When two people are playing Passing, they are as animated as the ball—bending, dipping, stretching, turning, twisting, running forward, running back, all with the aim of keeping their athletic conversation going.

BUMP, SET, SPIKE

Players: 2
Area: Volleyball court
Equipment: Volleyball
Level of Difficulty:
Moderate

Bump, Set, Spike is a more complicated way to play volleyball catch. The net is not in play. Two players stand facing each other about ten to fifteen feet apart. The first player starts with a toss. The second player bumps or passes it back to the first, who "sets" it up into the air. The second player in turn spikes the ball to the first, who begins a new cycle with a pass. The reply to this pass is a set, followed by a spike, and round and round they go. The players may want to see how many passes they can make without a miscue.

CIRCLE GAME

Players: 5 or more
Area: Half a volleyball court
Equipment: Volleyball
Level of Difficulty: Moderate–advanced

Circle Game is another way to encourage volleyball communication—rather than a one-on-one dialogue as with Bump, Set, Spike, it requires group interaction.

The circle can expand or contract depending on the number of players involved. The central figure is the setter, who will more than likely be a parent or coach. The setter distributes the ball around the circle so everyone gets a crack at bumping and digging and sliding and hollering and saving the ball from that worst of fates: hitting the floor. The players must keep the ball in the air, and contests can be arranged to see how many times a group can hit it without losing control.

Start with a high toss to the setter, who taps it to someone in the circle. Every ball comes back to the setter. The setter then sets it for someone else, and around and around it goes. The setter positions herself with her back to the net in the center of the floor. Volleyball being the game it is, however, it will not be long before the ball starts flying all over the place—anywhere but to the setter. Someone in the circle must then jump forward to save the ball—to keep it aloft and keep the game going.

Other ways to play: A more advanced version of Circle Game calls for five players: three passers, a setter, and a spiker. The setter sets to the spiker, who raps it in the direction of the passers, one of whom bumps it back to the setter, who sets it to the spiker, who raps it to another passer, etc.

PASS AND RUN

Players: Unlimited
Area: Volleyball court
Equipment: Volleyball
Level of Difficulty: Moderate

Pass and Run is a simple passing weave. Start with two single-file lines of players, with the children at the head of each line facing each other three or four feet away. One player tosses to the other to start the game, then runs to the end of the opposite line. The other child responds with a pass, and runs to the end of the line opposite him. The next player bumps the ball in turn and runs to the end of the opposite line. And so on.

The coach may want to give the players a goal to shoot for: say, six (or eight or ten) passes in a row without a miscue. Before play commences, the instruction should be: Pass, then go right. But a coach should never let his players get stuck in a rut. So, after a period of time, throw them a curve: Pass, and go left.

Other ways to play: A popular variation of Pass and Run brings the net into play. This game is similar to Around the World in tennis, and is more suited for older players. The two teams face each other across the net. They must pass the ball over the net to one another, then negotiate their way under and around the net as they run breathlessly to the opposite line.

THE SERVING GAME

Players: 2 teams of 3 or more
Area: Volleyball court
Equipment: Volleyball
Level of Difficulty: Moderate

The Serving Game can help teach kids one of the toughest aspects of volleyball: the serve. Divide the group into two teams, with each team on either side of the net. There is no return of serve in this game; a point is scored simply if a player succeeds in hitting a fair serve. This is not so easy for younger players. But it can seem less daunting—and their confidence in their abilities can grow—by the simple technique of moving the serving line closer in.

Start the hitting five feet from the back line. If a player hits his serve over the net and it lands in bounds on the opposite side, he scores 1 point for his team. After one team hits, the other team, which has been retrieving balls during this time, gets its chance. Then each team moves in five feet and tries again. Then another five feet. The team with the most points after four or so rounds is the champ.

When they're starting out, younger players should serve underhanded. Later, when they become stronger and more skilled, they can try overhand. The sequence of the Serving Game can also be reversed, beginning with the easier attempts closer to the net and gradually moving out toward the back line.

THREE-ON-THREE-ON-THREE

Players: Teams of 3
Area: Volleyball court
Equipment: Volleyball
Level of Difficulty: Advanced

Three-on-Three-on-Three is a fast, free-flowing game. The coach, who controls the pace of the game, throws the ball in from the side to a team of three. They can bump, pass, spike, do anything—just keep the ball off the floor and get it over the net. The opposing team does the same. They play 1-point matches. When one team loses, it scrambles off the court to be quickly replaced by another threesome waiting in the wings. The coach quickly launches the ball, and a new game commences.

Hitting the first ball back is forbidden; a team that does that automatically loses the point and the game. Players must pass at least two times, and for younger players, three passes is better still.

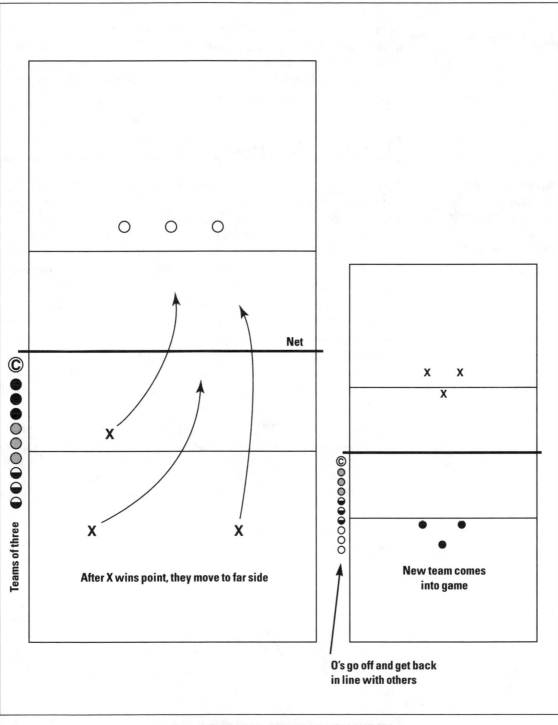

Teams of three

Net

After X wins point, they move to far side

New team comes
into game

O's go off and get back
in line with others

THREE-ON THREE-ON THREE-VOLLEYBALL

The winning team always sets up on the far court, across the net from the coach-server. As long as a team wins it stays on the court. But when it gets beaten the conquering team rushes across into the open court and takes over. It then faces a new set of challengers across from it. If one team begins to dominate, the coach—that crafty soul—can deftly move them off with a hard-to-handle serve.

BEACH VOLLEYBALL (DOUBLES)

Players: 4 or more
Area: Beach
Equipment: Volleyball, portable net
Level of Difficulty: Advanced

Beach Volleyball is cool. In its most popular form, Beach Volleyball is doubles—two people on a side. But three, four, five, or more on a side can play this game. Beach Volleyball is, in fact, more than a game; it's a lifestyle. And everybody is invited.

Normally in volleyball the more players there are, the more strategy is involved. Doubles on the beach requires strategy, but it is more of a partnership thing. The best doubles teams have played together before. They know their partner's moves and can anticipate where the other is going to be and what he or she is going to do in a given situation. When one player itches, the other scratches.

Beach Volleyball is most fun with coed teams (and cross-generational, if it's a family outing). If playing doubles, the game is You-Me-You and over the net. Teammates must get actively involved, else they'll be watching from the sidelines in short order.

Sand is a terrific medium for volleyball expression. The sand gives away underfoot, and players cannot move as fast as they can on a court. But unlike the less forgiving hardwood floors where they usually play, expert volleyballers can stretch out in the air and really give up their bodies. These players dive for balls like pelicans diving for fish. Beach Volleyball is a barefoot game. Scratch out the court boundaries with your toes, and serve it up. Games are to 15. Losers have to put suntan lotion on the winners' backs.

TWO-SPORT GAMES

Another name for this chapter might be Hybrid Games. Hybrid or two-sport games take the elements of one sport and graft them onto another, forming something quite novel and fun. Two-sport games are an excellent teaching approach. They can combine a familiar sport (such as baseball) with one that youngsters may still be learning (like tennis or swimming). Soccer is specially suited for two-sport games, perhaps because it is not as well known in this country as other sports. Soccer instructors often must work to build bridges with their young pupils, who may never have seen a soccer game in their lives.

The two-sport games in this chapter may also serve as inspiration for coaches looking for new games to teach and play. Is there a way to create a different game by incorporating elements from one or two other sports into your own? Games are interconnected, after all, and the basic skills of athletics—running, jumping, throwing—are universal in sports.

Basketball

PIN BASKETBALL

Players: Unlimited, divided into 2 teams
Area: Basketball court
Equipment: 2 basketballs, 1 bowling pin
Level of Difficulty: Easy–moderate

Pin Basketball is essentially a free-throw shooting game. But the introduction of a quirky, incongruous element—a bowling pin—adds a fun twist.

The two teams line up at half court. One person on each team begins the game by rolling a basketball and trying to knock down the bowling pin located underneath the basket. It's about a half-court roll, performed one player at a time. If both players miss, the next persons in line try until somebody nails the pin. Strike!

The team whose player knocks down the pin moves up to the free-throw line and shoots free throws—one free throw per person. Every free throw made equals 1 point for the team. To keep busy during this period, the players on the other team should break into two lines at half court and practice chest passes, moving the ball rapidly back and forth between them.

After the free-throw shooting finishes, the two teams meet again at half court for another bowl-off. When the pin gets toppled, that team moves up to the free-throw line, and the process is repeated. The team that earns the most free-throw shooting points wins.

Hockey

HOCKEY BASEBALL

Players: 6–10
Area: Ice rink (or with in-line skates, playground)
Equipment: Skates, hockey sticks for each player, hockey gloves, puck, 3 traffic cones, goal net
Level of Difficulty: Moderate

Hockey Baseball marries the national sport of Canada with the national sport of the United States. The game observes baseball rules, but instead of batting around a ball, the players shoot a puck.

The game requires a minimum of three players; a "pitcher," a "batter," and at least one "outfielder." The rink is the field. The pitcher begins the action by passing the puck to the batter waiting in front of the net. The batter catches the puck and shoots it back past the pitcher to wherever he can get it to go. Then the batter takes off to first base just as if he were trying to leg out a hit in baseball.

Set up three cones on the rink in the position of bases on a diamond—first, second, and third, with the net area serving as home. The batter advances while the outfielders skate after his puck and pass it back to the pitcher. An out is made if the batter hasn't reached first base by the time the pitcher brings the puck under control. Once the pitcher gains control of the puck, a runner who's safely made it to first or second must stay where he is. Just as in playground baseball, he must be advanced by the next person up.

Hockey Baseball teaches stick work and how to catch a pass. Large numbers of players can break into teams and play a game, keeping track of runs and advancing the runners just as they would in baseball. Or they can play a version of the baseball game One Old Cat (page 40), where the batter tries to run from home to first and back again before the puck gets returned to the pitcher. If he doesn't make it, he is out and a new person gets to hit. Or the fielders could try to shoot the puck directly at the hitter as he's running; hit him and he's out (in this case a tennis ball should be substituted for a puck).

Soccer Hockey

Players: 2 teams of 3 or more
Area: Ice rink
Equipment: Skates, hockey gloves, soccer ball, goal net
Level of Difficulty: Moderate

In Soccer Hockey, players put their sticks away. The rules of soccer apply—no using the hands!—and each team tries to kick the ball into the other team's net and score points. Kicking around a soccer ball while on ice skates is a sure method of improving coordination and balance.

Kickball Hockey

Players: 2 teams of 3 or more
Area: Ice rink
Equipment: Skates, hockey gloves, hockey sticks, kickball, goal net
Level of Difficulty: Moderate

Kickball Hockey is another delightful commingling of games. Play it the same as schoolyard kickball, with two teams squaring off against each other using a baseball-style format. The pitcher rolls the ball up to the plate, and the kicker kicks it as hard and as far as he can. Coaches might insert a slightly heavier ball than a soccer ball into this game, so that the ball isn't flying all over the place.

Soccer

SKITTLES (SOCCER BOWLING)

Players: 2–10
Area: Soccer field
Equipment: 10 traffic cones, soccer balls
Level of Difficulty: Easy

Skittles is bowling with a kick. Arrange ten cones in a triangular shape, just as they do the pins in alley bowling. Make the kicking distance ten feet or ten yards, whatever is appropriate. The players must kick with the side of their foot, as always, and knock down the cones. As few as two players can play Skittles, but it's also a good team game. Each team has its own set of cones. Players rotate turns, taking one kick apiece. The team that knocks down all the pins first, wins.

SOCCER TENNIS

Players: 2 or 4
Area: Tennis court with net
Equipment: Soccer ball
Level of Difficulty: Easy–moderate

Soccer Tennis is for younger players. Players bat the ball back and forth by kicking or heading it over the net. Younger players generally have a hard time controlling the ball, and the larger area of a tennis court gives them room to make mistakes. (Or set up a version of the game on a soccer field and give them even more room.) For those who are just learning to dribble and kick, play in the style of the tennis game Anything Goes (page 161)—letting the ball bounce repeatedly after it crosses the net. Players gather the ball up, bring it back, and comfortably bop it across the net to the other side.

SOCCER CROQUET

Players: Unlimited
Area: Soccer field, grassy area
Equipment: Traffic cones, soccer ball for each player
Level of Difficulty: Easy–moderate

In regular croquet, players hit balls with mallets through wire wickets. In Soccer Croquet, players kick soccer balls between traffic cones. The difficulty of the course and the distance between the cones depends on the skills of the players. Lay out the course in the same way as ordinary croquet, so that players work their way down to a halfway point, turn around, and return home.

Players can play one-on-one, or on two-person teams (with each person taking turns), or as a group. One element remains constant: As in lawn croquet, everyone has the right to knock someone else's ball with their own ball as far as they can. Boys and girls just *love* that.

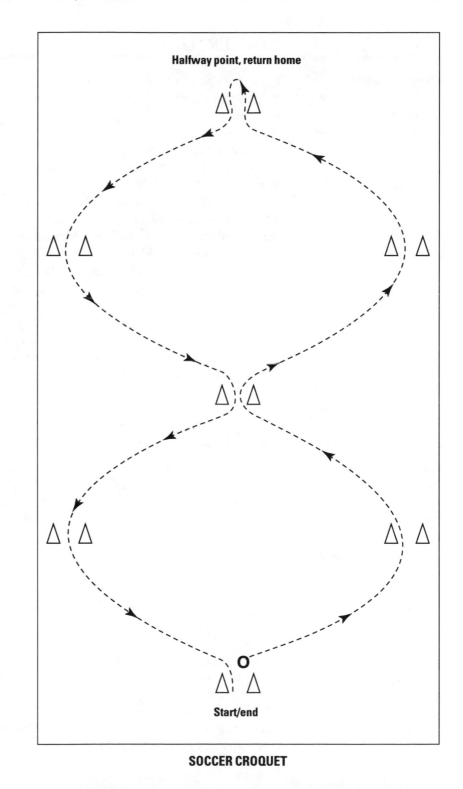

Halfway point, return home

Start/end

SOCCER CROQUET

SOCCER GOLF

Players: Unlimited
Area: Soccer field and
environs
Equipment: Soccer ball
for each player
Level of Difficulty:
Easy–moderate

Soccer Golf is most fun when it is all over the map. Do not restrict players to the soccer field. Let them go everywhere, and shoot at anything.

Everyone has a ball. The number of holes can vary, although ideally each player gets a chance to pick a hole and determine the number of strokes it will take to reach it. Most Soccer Golf holes are par 3s, although an exceptionally long and difficult hole could require five strokes.

One stroke equals one kick. The holes can be almost anything—the inside of a garbage can, a goalpost, the coach's Maxima (well, maybe not), a wall, the doors of a building, *through* the doors of a building: Let the imagination of the players lead the way. Once a hole is established, players can shoot all at once—that's a wild sight, thirty balls flying in the air toward an open garbage can—or one at a time, in the traditional golf manner. One player shoots, then the next, trading turns until each puts the ball where it is supposed to go.

If they wish, the players can keep track of their scores to see who scored par or better on the course. Or the winner can be the person who shoots the best on the very last hole.

SOCCER BASEBALL

Players: 2 teams of 5 or
more
Area: Soccer field
Equipment: Soccer ball
Level of Difficulty:
Moderate–advanced

All ages and ability levels can play Soccer Baseball. For the younger ages, it may somewhat resemble old-fashioned kickball, but the fact that none of the players can touch the ball with their hands makes for a crucial difference. The game should be played on a soccer field, with one of the goalposts serving as home base.

A pitcher rolls a ball up to the "batter," who boots it soccer-style as far as he can. He runs around the bases while the fielders try to collect the ball (no hands!) and get him out. The game can be played different ways, but the most common version has the batter circling the bases after a kick. The fielders try to kick the ball into the net before the runner rounds all the bases. If they kick it into the net before he reaches home, the runner is out; if the runner makes it safely all the way around the bases, he scores a point for his team.

Soccer Baseball can be made more difficult for advanced players by giving the people in the field certain requirements. Each fielder, for instance, might be required to make a specified number of touches—decided upon by the coach—before he can pass the ball. The skill of the player should determine the level of challenge. One person may only have to do a header before passing it on; another may be asked to juggle with his feet, thigh, and head.

Another requirement could be that all fielders must touch the ball after the batter kicks it—no quick shots to catch the runner. If there are six fielders, they must make six passes. The time it takes to make their passes—as well as the requirement to make a certain number of touches —should give the runner a sporting chance to hit a soccer home run. The fielders cannot, however, shoot at the net from any point closer than the penalty line—twelve yards out. They can shoot again if they miss the goal, but the runner is usually running so hard that there is seldom time for a second shot.

SOCCER VOLLEYBALL

Players: 2 teams of 6 or more
Area: Volleyball court with net
Equipment: Soccer ball
Level of Difficulty: Advanced

While the younger children are playing Soccer Tennis, the older, more advanced players can play Soccer Volleyball. Play it almost like volleyball—the primary difference being, of course, that a soccer ball is used, not a volleyball. Players cannot use their hands. They must return and pass with their feet or head, practicing headers and short volley kicks. As in volleyball, the ball cannot hit the ground (or only once), else the serving team scores a point. Players may touch the ball three times on a side before returning it back over the net. Soccer Volleyball is great for teaching ball control and helping foster communication among teammates.

Swimming

WATER BASEBALL

Players: 2 or more
Area: Swimming pool
Equipment: Kickboard, tennis ball
Level of Difficulty: Easy

Play baseball in the pool—why not? Use a kickboard as a bat and a tennis ball as the old horsehide. Two people with imagination can easily play by themselves, or teams with lots of players can face off. In the former version, one person hits, the other pitches. They will probably elect not to run the bases, determining hits and outs based on where the ball lands (just as in the baseball game Over the Line). Or, if there are two teams playing against each other, they may set up the bases and boundaries and play regulation ball. Batters swim, fielders swim, everybody swims.

WATER FOOTBALL

Players: 6–10
Area: Swimming pool
Equipment: Nerf or
rubber football
Level of Difficulty:
Easy–moderate

Like Water Baseball, Water Football is a fun game for children because they are already familiar with the popular sport and won't be intimidated when they play it in a pool. They can play two-handed touch football, or tackle. Tackle, although a bit more rugged, has advantages in that the players get knocked off their feet underwater and must spring back up to the surface. If they have any lingering anxieties about the water, this will help overcome them.

WATER BASKETBALL

Players: 2 or more
Area: Swimming pool
Equipment: Light ball,
basket
Level of Difficulty:
Moderate

Sports specialty stores and department stores sell portable basketball hoops that can be attached to the deck of a pool. Water Basketball is somewhat similar to Water Polo, especially as the game moves into deeper water. It builds up the legs and lungs and because there is so much feinting and faking, it may even improve a player's talents when he leaves the water and moves his game to the playground.

WATER VOLLEYBALL

Players: 2 teams of 2 or
more
Area: Swimming pool
Equipment: Water polo
ball, backstroke
flags line
Level of Difficulty:
Moderate–advanced

Yet another sport that translates wonderfully to an aquatic environment, Water Volleyball is simple to set up. One doesn't even need a net. Instead, string the backstroke flags line across the pool. Although very high off the water, it works quite well.

Play strict volleyball rules—three hits to a side, only the serving team can score—or variations on them. Players may want to catch the ball after receiving it, rather than hitting it. Allow three passes on each side before the ball has to go back over the net. If somebody misses a catch and the ball falls to the water, that is a point for the other side. If a serve drops over the rope untouched, that's also a point. A player may smother a ball and go underwater with it, but he must come back up with it under control; if he does not, that is a point for the other side, too. Teams must win by 2 points. The first team with 10 points, wins.

A water polo ball is recommended; it is a heavier ball and easier to control and catch. Lighter balls tend to bounce exasperatingly off the fingertips and even accomplished players have trouble handling them with any measure of dexterity.

Tennis

Tennis Baseball

Players: Unlimited
Area: Tennis court with net
Equipment: Tennis racket, balls
Level of Difficulty: Easy

Tennis Baseball is for tennis rookies. The pitcher (usually the coach or instructor) lobs the ball softly in to the batter, who is standing on the end line. If and when he makes contact—the game is designed to encourage that, to help him relax and hit—he takes off around "the bases." The right side of the net could be first base, the left side of the net second, etc. While the child runs around the court in high gear, the fielders chase the ball down and attempt to throw him out.

Another version of Tennis Baseball gives the batter a hit based on where the ball lands. Batters do not run. If the ball lands in the left service box, it is ruled a single; if it lands in the right service box, it is a double. A triple is any batted ball that falls between the service lines and the baseline. Teammates try to move one another around the bases and score runs, much like in the traditional baseball game of Over the Line. A single moves a runner on first base up to second, another single moves him to third, etc. Any ball that is struck into the net or out of play beyond the lines of the court is an out. Three net or out balls equal three outs, and the batting team takes the field and the fielding team comes in to hit. (Illustration is on next page.)

Volleyball

Hand Soccer

Players: Teams of 3 or more
Area: Volleyball court without net
Equipment: Volleyball
Level of Difficulty: Easy–moderate

Hand Soccer is a good warm-up game for volleyball. Put goals at each end of the court (a goal might consist of two knee pads placed five or six feet apart). There are no goalies, and kicking the ball is not allowed. Players practice ball awareness as they bat the ball with one hand. There are two teams, and a point is scored when one of the teams shoots the volleyball through the goal. The ball moves quickly around the court mainly by passing. Players backpedal, bend, stretch, cut, and move with agility. They play the whole court, run up and down and up and down, and work up a nice, light sweat before the volleyball starts for real.

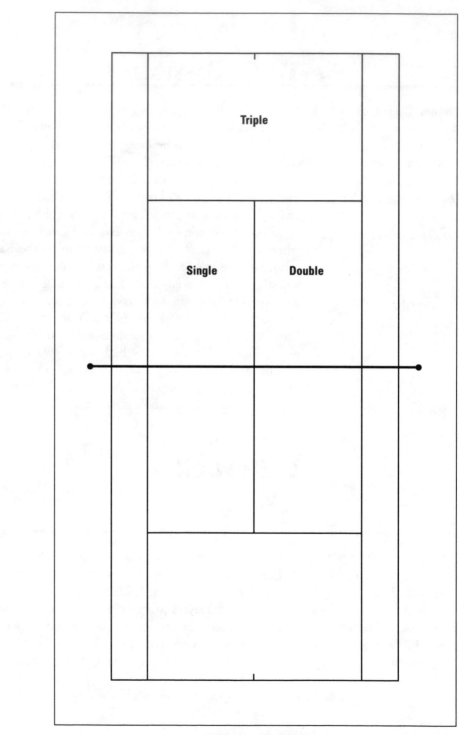

TENNIS BASEBALL

SIXTEEN

MISCELLANEOUS FUN GAMES

Not every sports-derived game can be neatly categorized by sport. Some games use skills from one, two, or three sports and yet do not belong to any one of them. Here is a miscellaneous collection of games that allow children to use a variety of athletic skills in a variety of settings, while still having fun.

KICKBACK

Players: 11–20
Area: Playground basketball court
Equipment: Soccer ball (or playground ball)
Level of Difficulty: Easy

Kickback contains elements of kickball and basketball, but is its own unique game. Two teams play on a playground basketball court. The pitcher stands at the top of the key (or thereabouts), with her team arrayed in the field behind her. If there are enough players, somebody should act as catcher too. The pitcher rolls the ball to the kicker, who stands to one side of the basketball pole and kicks from about the baseline. This sets the contest in motion.

The kicker runs clockwise around the basketball half-court area, sticking to the lines. A round-tripper concludes at the basketball pole. There are no singles or doubles; it's a home run or nothing in Kickback. While the kicker races madly around the court, the players in the field round up the ball and try to shoot it in the basket. That is how to get a person out: by shooting the ball into the basket before the runner has completed the circuit and slapped the pole with her hand. If the runner makes it all the way, she scores a point for her team. Three outs to a side, as in baseball.

TETHERBALL

Players: 2
Area: Playground
Equipment: Tetherball and pole
Level of Difficulty: Easy

Tetherball is a fixture of many American playgrounds. Grade schoolers still play it, and why not? It is fun and fast and the rules are easily understood. Basically, each player tries to wrap the ball completely around the pole by batting or hitting it with his hand. The ball whips around high and fast as the one player tries to keep it going his way and the other struggles to block it and turn it around the other way. One person can control the ball, not letting the other get a hit, if he is able. The person who wraps the ball around the pole going in his direction wins.

Though it is a playground game, tetherball resembles volleyball in many respects; it's basically volleyball on a rope. Blocking a tetherball conveys some of the same satisfaction volleyball players must feel when they spring high above the net to block an opponent's spike. Take that! Unlike volleyball, players can catch and throw the ball, though they cannot touch the rope except on the first throw of the game. Snagging the rope as a means of stopping the ball is against the rules and gives the other player a free throw or hit.

RELAY RACES

Players: Unlimited
Area: Playground or field
Equipment: None
Level of Difficulty: All levels

Before they shone in the Olympics, Carl Lewis and Florence Joyner no doubt shone on the playground. Running is one of the joys of being young. Relay races not only allow children to experience this joy in a group setting, but they also help build strong legs and healthy hearts. Teams of three or more can compete against one another. The distances they run depend on their ages and the area of play.

Never let children themselves pick the teams; a parent, teacher, or coach should do that. And if a coach really wants to wear the group out, try continuous relays; after a team of four runs its legs, the anchor person ("anchor" or last person in line) hands off to the first or lead-off person, and they go *again*. Running races are an especially refreshing event for grade school children, because at this age the girls can compete equally with boys and frequently surpass them.

Paper, Rock, Scissors (Athletic Version)

Players: Unlimited
Area: Open area, volleyball court with net
Equipment: None
Level of Difficulty: Easy–moderate

The well-known game of Paper, Rock, Scissors gets an athletic spin. Although ideal for volleyball because it promotes togetherness and team harmony in a fun way, it is perfectly suited to other sports and situations as well. Players must make split-second decisions, and the amount of running they do makes this game an excellent (and fun) conditioning builder.

Divide the players into two teams. The two teams huddle up and decide, in secret, which they want: paper (flat hand), rock (fist), or scissors (index and forefinger). The teams line up across from one another with a line dividing them (or the net, if playing on a volleyball court).

On a count of three, the players all reveal at the same time the sign their team has chosen. If one team beats the other—chooses paper to the other's rock, etc.—the winning members turn and run to a pre-established point ten or so feet beyond the back line of the court. If all of these players make it safely to this area, that team wins. But that's not as easy as it sounds.

Firstly, a member of the losing team may save its team by capturing one of the winners running back to the safe area. If she does indeed catch him before he reaches this point, the game is a wash. Nobody wins, and the teams huddle up again and pick another sign. If both teams pick the same sign, that counts for nothing and the teams must rehuddle.

This athletic version of Paper Rock Scissors forces the players to make split-second decisions. They must first recognize the sign and decide whether their team has won or lost, and react. Many make wrong choices or get utterly mixed up, and it is altogether normal to see winners mistakenly chasing losers, and losers running away thinking they've won, and all sorts of joyful confusion. And the players get a good workout without even noticing it.

Wall Ball (Throwing)

Players: 2
Area: Playground with wall or board
Equipment: Tennis ball
Level of Difficulty: Easy–moderate

Two players vie against each other in this throwing and catching game. One player throws a tennis ball that must bounce on the ground before it hits the wall. The other player must in turn catch it on the rebound before it bounces three times. If the ball bounces three times (or more), the catcher is out and if there are others waiting to play, the next person in line is in. If, however, the catcher catches the ball on the fly, the thrower is out. When the ball bounces just one or two times, neither person wins and they keep on playing.

Kickball

Players: 11–20
Area: Playground or field
Equipment: Kickball
Level of Difficulty: Moderate

Kickball is a kind of soccer baseball. A pitcher rolls the ball on the ground to the batter/kicker, who runs the bases after making contact. All one needs to play this game is a large round rubber ball—not a bat or a hoop or a racket or a goal or even bases. Just a ball, a good strong set of legs, and the will to kick.

Kickball is played on a baseball diamond, with the defenders arrayed in their positions like baseball fielders. They retrieve the ball and do their utmost to get the team at the plate out. The kicker cannot run too far past home plate when he kicks; if he does he is out. Some kickball games stipulate that runners must be tagged out or the ball must beat them to the base, as in baseball. Others play that if the fielders get the ball back to the pitcher in time, the runner is out. Still others say that the fielders may throw at the runner and if they hit him between the bases with the ball, he is out. Throwing at a runner above the waist is never allowed, however. Three outs to a side, as in baseball.

Whatever rules one plays by, it is imperative to establish rules *of some kind.* Some kids with an urge to kick may get together and begin to play, but if they do not establish a few simple tenets first—what is a fair and foul ball, where second base actually is, how to get a person out, etc.—the game will inevitably degenerate into arguments and tantrums, followed by one or more of the players storming off in a self-righteous huff.

WALL BALL (KICKING)

Players: 2
Area: Playground with wall or board
Equipment: Playground ball
Level of Difficulty: Moderate–advanced

Instead of throwing a tennis ball as in the throwing version of Wall Ball, players kick a playground ball against a wall. There are various ways to play. The simplest version is like the throwing game. Kickers kick the ball back and forth against the wall. If a person kicks the ball twice in a row—meaning he has mishandled it in some way—he is out. Kicking out of bounds or missing the wall will also knock a player out.

A more advanced version of the game builds soccer skills. After striking the wall the ball can bounce any number of times on the rebound; that doesn't matter. What does matter in this game is what the player does after he collects the ball. He cannot "touch" the ball more than two times as he gathers it up to kick it back against the wall. A touch is defined as any contact with the body (except the hands). Three touches and he's out. This rule may be relaxed for younger players to allow more touches.

As in soccer, players cannot use their hands; they have to control the ball only with their feet and other parts of their body. A person is out if he uses his hands, touches three times, or misses the wall when he kicks. For this reason using a board or narrow strip of wood as the backstop is more challenging than a wall; it creates a much harder target to shoot for.

TEAM HANDBALL

Players: 14 or more
Area: Basketball court
Equipment: Nets for goals, playground ball
Level of Difficulty: Moderate–advanced

Team Handball is actually a sport in its own right. Originating in Europe in the late 1920s, it took forty years before it arrived on this continent. Now the United States Team Handball Federation, based in Boulder, Colorado, supervises the sport in this country. Team Handball is an Olympic sport for men and women and claims to be the second most popular sport in Europe behind soccer.

In this country, Team Handball is primarily a school game. If a big future awaits Team Handball in the United States, it is being created today by P.E. teachers introducing their students (and vice versa) to this fast-moving, fast-shooting game. Team Handball at its best makes basketball look slow and stodgy.

Team Handball is easily adapted to a basketball court. Set the goals up at either end of the court under each basket. A goal is approximately seven feet high by ten feet wide. It is not strictly necessary to have nets to play Team Handball, but it is nice. As the sport's literature points out, "Try to imagine using a peach basket for a basketball goal today." Fling-

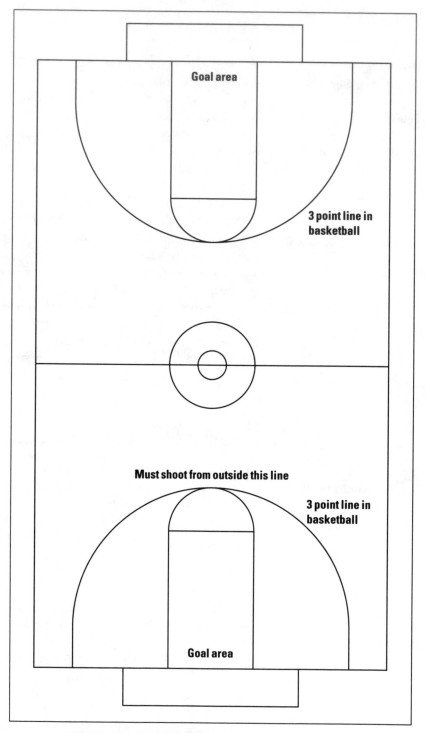

Goal area

3 point line in
basketball

Must shoot from outside this line

3 point line in
basketball

Goal area

TEAM HANDBALL (ADAPTED TO BASKETBALL COURT)

ing the ball past the goal and "ripping the net" is one of the chief thrills of the game.

The Olympic game stipulates seven players on a side—six court players, one goalie—but the nature of most P.E. classes inevitably dictates more bodies per team. Team Handball includes elements of basketball, water polo, soccer, and hockey. Players must run, jump, catch, and throw a playground ball, while trying to fake out their defenders and rip the net. Each goal is 1 point. A game is divided into halves. It begins with the coach or instructor tossing the ball into play. At halftime the teams switch goals, and a game lasts until it is time to go into the locker room and get changed.

Team Handball is a misnomer; the game bears almost no resemblance to ordinary handball. Players flow up and down the court in near-constant motion. In the playground version of the game, players do not stick to "positions" per se; they're all over the place. There is great beauty and style to the game, especially when a player leaps acrobatically into the air to launch a shot or, faking that, tosses the ball up for a teammate coming in behind him who spears it in the air and slams it past the goalie into the net in one continuous motion. No wonder the kids have picked up on this game.

Team Handball emphasizes teamwork. Players can pass in any direction. Indeed, the pass—as opposed to the dribble—is the recommended means of ball transport. Beginners should only dribble once or twice before passing. Lots of passing keeps the ball zipping around, gets everybody involved, and keeps the game moving. A player can run three steps with the ball before letting a shot go. The legality of "air dribbling"—passing to yourself as a means of advancing the ball—is best decided by local jurisdiction. Technically the rules forbid it, but some generous-spirited P.E. teachers allow one air ball per possession. If a player gets stopped, he is allowed to toss the ball in the air as a way of keeping his momentum going.

Fouls are called and free throws awarded. Fouls are called for reaching in, excessive physical contact, and other offenses. The free throw is taken right away, from the spot of the infraction. Players cannot hit the ball out of someone's hands. There is no kicking or rolling the ball, although some hot-shots do bounce their shots into goal. As in soccer or hockey, the goal area is off limits to all but the goalie, and the shooters must fire away from behind the 3-point line on a basketball court, or about nineteen feet.

DOG PATCH OLYMPICS

Players: Unlimited

Area: Athletic field, camp, woods, park

Equipment: Whatever the task requires

Level of Difficulty: All levels

Dog Patch Olympics is the quintessential outdoor sports game, because no special equipment is required and nothing needs to be brought from home. Everything that is used may be found on the spot, or created there. Nor does one need to be anywhere special to hold a Dog Patch Olympics. It can take place in the woods, in a big field or park, or around the neighborhood. Camp is a prime spot because different sporting environments—swimming pool, basketball courts, rec hall, field—are usually on site.

There is no such thing as a "typical" Dog Patch Olympics; every Dog Patch Olympics is unique. It may include such events as a free-throw shooting contest, a swim race, a long-distance football toss, an accuracy baseball throw, soccer kicking, a running race, and standing long-jump, high-jump, and gymnastic-type balance contests. But the games need not be traditional athletic games. They could be anything from a sack race or a wheelbarrow race to wiggle walking or crawling like a snake in the grass, to walking across a log and climbing a tree. Or it could be a mix of traditional and nontraditional. Dog Patch Olympics is another way of saying "Whatever works."

Players may compete individually, but clearly, dividing into teams and holding relay races are the most satisfying way to stage a Dog Patch Olympics. One way to make the competition even more fun is to make the participants carry something—a sock, say, or a spoon—on their person as they're doing the event. If they drop it at some point along the way they've got to go back and get it. They pass the object on when they reach the next person in the relay. Enjoy!

ACKNOWLEDGMENTS

Anyone who despairs for the future of these United States should spend some time talking with the players, coaches, and parents who are involved with youth sports in this country. Despite some problems, sports remains one of the most positive environments for young people today. In writing and researching this book I was lucky to meet many fine people who generously shared their time and expertise with me.

I owe a special thanks to Charlie Hoeveler, who allowed me to attend several of his excellent US Sports youth athletic camps. At these camps a number of coaches and instructors shared their best teaching games with me. They included Dick Gould, Marc Haddad, Dave Welz, Steve Pence, and Sara Halleck. Reamy Goodwin was a fount of goodwill and suggestions. For my chapter on volleyball I relied on the special contributions of Jim Cherniss and Dean Sutcliffe. Al Rodriguez, John Kosty, and Don Shaw were also helpful to me.

One of the most gifted basketball teachers I encountered was Tony Ronzone. Leo Williams, Steve Coccimiglio, past Hayward High basketball coach Joe Fuccy, and current Hayward coach Charlie Kendall all contributed basketball games. Another fine Hayward athletic coach, Jim Bisenius, now retired, went out of his way to help me with his specialty of baseball. Rob Andrews was also kind enough to let me attend one of the San Francisco Giants baseball camps that he operates.

Karl Dewazien, who has written several fine books on soccer, graciously allowed me to attend a California Youth Soccer Association coaches' clinic. There, I met Tim Barr, Ken Mitchell, and Mary Moxley, all of whom contributed games. Geoff Smyth, coach of the Las Positas Community College girls soccer team, was a great boon. Robin Tanner of the North American Soccer Camps and Dan McCormick also were very helpful to me.

Teachers were a big source of information and inspiration: John Tsubota, Dan Witters, Jim Travis, Charlene McNally, Sheila Nelson, and several teachers sitting around the lunch table at Canyon Middle School in Castro Valley, California, all made valuable contributions.

Ken Johnson proved an invaluable resource for hockey games. Johnson and Elysse Soll of the San Jose Sharks allowed me to attend one of the Sharks' hockey camps, which increased my understanding of the sport. The chapter on swimming games could not have been done without the help of Mark and Matt Croghan. Marcia (nee Croghan) Bergendahl and Steve Bergendahl also made valuable suggestions. Sherry Endicott and Rosalie Casals gave me tennis games. Jay Dennis, Wes Dennis, Jack Renfro, Gene Gire, and the Benicia High athletic department contributed to the football chapter.

I am proud to say that many young people also contributed games to this book. They included Robert Converse, David and Daniel Maggart, Robert Pace, Trevor and Troy Croghan, Nicole Bergendahl, and Annie Nelson. Jeff Williams and David Sheldon, two precocious young Canadian golfers, filled me in on the games they like to play. Katie and Kristy Nelson and I spent a pleasant evening together taking about games over a takeout dinner from Burger King.

Many more people shared their memories and game-playing experiences with me. They included Dan Crouch, Gary Grillo, Steve Bragonier, Laurie Odell, Marde Nelson, Anne Ewing, Mike and Becky Maggart, Eric Hansen, Midge Norry, Kenneth Lee, Scott Thomason, Dan Gelineau of the Harker Summer Camps of San Jose, Matt Hart, Kay Ray, Jack Ruszel, Jim Taranto, and Scott Christiansen. My sincerest apologies if I have left anyone out. Any errors in the text are entirely mine.

—KEVIN NELSON

INDEX

GAMES BY SPORT OR ACTIVITY

Games by the number of participants who can play it

(Compiled with the understanding that many games for one, two, three, or four players can also work with groups, and that games for lots of people or an unlimited number may be played with fewer participants too.)

ABOUT THE AUTHOR

Kevin Nelson is a father, soccer coach, and class volunteer at his daughter's school. In addition, he has written seven books on sports. Nelson lives in the San Francisco Bay Area.